China: the
Last
Superpower

China: the Last Superpower

Joseph Lam
with
William Bray

New Leaf Press

First printing: January 1997
Second printing: April 1997

ISBN: 0-89221-343-4

Cover design by Steve Diggs & Friends, Nashville, TN

Dedication

To Nora Lam, my mother,
who suffered under the
power of the dragon
before I was born —
and escaped to tell about it.

Acknowledgments

I give special thanks to my wife, Susan, daughter Stephanie, and son Stephen, for their encouragement and love.

I also thank missionary journalist William Thomas Bray who collaborated closely with me on this timely book. A veteran foreign correspondent, he has covered Asia for over 30 years, and is an old China hand. Many times his voice and mine are blended into the editorial "I" — and we are friends as well as co-workers.

Thanks, also, to all the wonderful folks at New Leaf who helped produce and distribute this work. Without their help and sacrifice I wouldn't be able to give you this unique Chinese-American perspective ... a glimpse into your future in the coming world order.

— Joseph Lam

Contents

Preface

What next, America? What does the future hold as we face the awesome new reality looming on "our" Pacific Rim? It is no longer our lake. The USA has been caught by surprise. We now have to share our Pacific trading partners with a new giant. Asia is suddenly dominated by the Red Dragon of China — the world's last superpower.

"And what about Hong Kong?" This book is born against the urgent backdrop of Hong Kong's takeover by China. The dragon's power grab for this "Babylon on the Pacific" rivets global attention. And with good reason. What happens in Hong Kong over the coming decade will tell us much about our common futures — as Americans, as Chinese — as believers and non-believers alike.

It's questions like these that provoked New Leaf publisher Tim Dudley to sign me for this project. Advance orders for this book have been strong — a good sign that we're meeting the growing grassroots in America, demanding to know more about new China.

Why Are We Americans So Uneasy about China?

From outside, China appears to be a lot like a swarming hive of one billion "worker bees" — and it looks scary. The average American has an uneasy feeling about China in general. He doesn't know how to deal with the Red Dragon — and understands little of what's happening in the East.

I've written *China: The Last Superpower* for this man or woman. It's not written just for diplomats, missionaries, scholars, soldiers, or spies. Instead, I am answering the real questions you are asking about New China today:

> — Why is China re-arming for both conventional and nuclear war?
> — Why has China become our main trading partner?
> — Why can't our government do something about slave labor and human rights in China?
> — Who is really running China?
> — What's behind China's love/hate relationship with the USA?

I have written this book to empower you to face the coming Asian century with confidence — to go beyond CNN sound bites and other headline news to make sense of our collective tomorrow. As a Chinese American, I also want to provide you with some basic background on my 5,000-year-old culture and history . . . and insight into the spiritual forces that control the Chinese people.

Surprising Rebirth of Communism

For most Americans, who believed the media reports that communism was dead, it's a shock to see it being "reborn" in Hong Kong! This wasn't supposed to happen. What's more, this brand of communism is not the old, discredited Marxism of the USSR. It is a new, far more powerful and more pragmatic force than ever before.

China's new communism has a savvy, market attitude that is beating capitalism at its own game. But this book is not meant to be an anti-Communist polemic — I believe something far more sinister than communism is at work in China today. Communism is not our enemy, but the force behind it is.

A strong, new China has emerged from the cold war years. It is not only the biggest and fastest-growing economy in the world — it is ominously aggressive and tired of the old restraints. China is testing its new power. Standing up. Saying "no" to the West.

China in Bible Prophecy

Who's really behind this expansionism? The answer is surprising. As always, current events are clearly explained by Bible predictions. God's Word has the answers we need for all our tomorrows. But I'm not trying to change anybody's eschatology in this book. It won't hurt my feelings if you don't accept my interpretations of Bible prophecy!

I have only included the place of China and the dragon in Bible prophecy to better share my urgency . . . why I am so concerned now for my people. The saddest sight on earth today is behind the new Bamboo Curtain — 1.2 billion suffering souls moving relentlessly toward death and destruction.

This new Bamboo Curtain is high tech, shiny, and even luxurious — but it still hides the horrors of Tiananmen Square and a vast network of 1,100 "Laogai" slave labor camps. Most of all, it hides a new imperialism far bigger than merely old-fashioned communism on the march.

Dealing with the Dragon

The Great Dragon is emerging from China for his final desperate gamble — global conquest. It will lead to the world war to end all wars. And before that it will introduce a frightening one-world economy, religion, and government. This is his final attempt at world conquest, and China is his last superpower. His Armageddon trump card.

Hong Kong's takeover appears to bode ill for peace and freedom around the world, but this may not always be the case. "Hong Kong/China" is the new epicenter of world trade. The doors and windows of freedom are going to slam both open and shut there in days ahead. Ditto for China. These are classic Chinese days of "crisis and opportunity" — a moment for Christian action.

Christians, don't dwell on the dark side of the future. We have the only hope for America and China. We have work to do — occupying until He comes. That's good news. I didn't write this book to shock or alarm you. I'm not afraid of the future. If this book scares you, use that fear to help you find Christ in these pages. Then you can face what's ahead without the dragon's terror.

A Personal Note

For me and my family, the future of China is very personal. I was miraculously born to my refugee mother, evangelist Nora Lam, in Hong Kong. It is still my second home. I have close family there, and frequently fly in and out of China. The island is an important base for much of our global humanitarian outreach. Hong Kong is not just the gateway to China, but to millions of other needy people in a host of Asian countries.

This book is meant to be a reality check for you, your family, and your various church groups. China and the USA have together entered a global age, locked into an unwilling embrace across the Pacific. I pray this book helps you make sense of the often crazy end-time world of China and the Pacific Rim.

Most of all, I hope this book helps us all stand strong — facing our future together in faith, not fear. I pray it makes you strong enough to love and be loved in the coming age of dis-information and hate. The Bible says "perfect love casts out fear." Without that love you can never hope to defeat the dragon and his end-time agenda for you and yours.

Joseph Lam
San Jose, California
January 1997

Chapter 1

Move Over America, the Jaws of the Dragon Are Open

> *Canst thou draw out leviathan with an hook? . . . Will he make a covenant with thee? . . . Upon earth there is not his like, who is made without fear* (Job 41:1–33).

C hina has re-emerged, center stage, on the global theater. After centuries of chaos, her billion workers are moving ahead with fresh national purpose. They are expectant with new hope — or horror — sometimes both at the same time!

Whenever experts talk of China in the 21st century, faces freeze. Conversation stops. Imaginations soar.

> • U.S. agricultural and commodities brokers grow smug, knowing that China tops the buyers list for everything they have — including Kansas wheat and Iowa corn.
> • American workers from California to

Michigan grow grim, knowing that every day, the United States exports more of their jobs and industry to China.

• Corporate chieftains in New York, Chicago, and Silicon Valley light up with glee as they scheme for a bigger share of the world's fastest growing economy.

• Military men in the Pentagon grow dark and silent, contemplating Beijing's drive to re-arm and modernize the biggest fighting machine on earth.

• Politicians and diplomats in Washington and at the United Nations seem puzzled, unsure about how to handle negotiations with our number one rival and trading partner.

• Bankers on Wall Street show alarm at the avalanche of U.S. capital and technology transferring to the other side of the Pacific.

• Economists puzzle about the growing imbalance of trade as China surpasses Japan and Europe as our biggest supplier!

• The U.S. treasury tries to stop the flow of red ink as our trade-debt to China grows greater every month.

• Tears come to the eyes of human rights activists as they monitor the bloody human toll of China's progress.

• Humanitarians struggle to save the growing tide of hurting children, women, and hungry adults who are victims of change.

• Bible scholars are re-discovering those texts that show the kings of the East holding the keys to understanding Armageddon and the day of the Lord.

Finally, mission-minded Christians hold their breath in awe at this change in the nations. For the Church on the verge of 21st century, the center of spiritual gravity is shifting from the United States to Asia. Revival is breaking out in Korea, India, and the Philippines. New fields are white unto harvest, yet hundreds of millions are still held in demonic bondage! China remains the largest of the closed cultures left on earth — the greatest single spiritual challenge we face.

Somewhere between 20-25 percent of the world's population is in Asia, and still has not freely heard the gospel. China is the keystone to reaching them; in fact, most are Chinese. For the bride of Christ, this is our last chance to get ready. This is the last crusade, the last frontier, the final spiritual obligation of the Church before her Master, the Lord Jesus Christ, returns.

The Challenge of China

Of course, the Lord Jesus Christ is not just another product to be delivered, nor is China merely a new market for the gospel. But it's hard to look at China without using marketing terms.

However, when it does come to goods and services, it is the mother of all markets — Babylon of all Babylons. Anytime you multiply a product by 1.2 billion hungry customers, you have a very, very big customer base! And the Chinese ethnic market extends far beyond the massive population within her borders. There are Chinese populations in every country of the world — often counted in the millions. No wonder China is the world's biggest economic trader — the largest mercantile nation on earth. This huge financial powerhouse is already the globe's biggest buyer of both capital and consumer goods.

This potential consumerism is the key to understanding America's long and mostly fruitless courtship with the Chinese. United States businesses, along with the rest of world, are panting to have economic access. But so far, the American love affair with Chinese communism has been a one-way street. The dragon continues to deny Americans access to Chinese consumer markets, preferring instead to import aircraft, capital, machine tools, manufacturing plants, technology, and weapons.

In 1996, we crossed an unprecedented economic divide with China. Our negative balance of trade with China became greater than any other nation on earth — surpassing Japan for the first time, and all of Europe combined! In the last month I checked before we went to press, the deficit was $4.73 billion, $1 billion more than our trade deficit with Japan for that month!

The Prophetic Puzzle of China

But for Bible scholars and students of prophecy, the appearance of this growing dragon in the East is a puzzle. Where does this new "monster-sized" nation fit into the end-times panorama?

China is a modern Goliath by any measurement. In spite of draconian mass murder through forced abortions, death camps, infanticide, and euthanasia—China's population is expected to reach 1.8 billion by 2020.

Over 93 percent of the population are of the Han race. Their Mandarin dialect is the official national language. However China is more diverse than it appears on the surface. There are 55 other ethnic minorities and tribes. Eight major languages are spoken, as well as over 600 regional dialects.

The country spans four time zones and sprawls over 3.7 million miles. It is the third largest country in the world behind Russia and Canada. It has 2,000 counties spread over 30 "states" which include 22 provinces, 5 autonomous regions, and 3 metropolitan districts. Outside the modern coastal cities with their soaring skylines are vast rural areas still primitive and ripe for economic development. It has three rivers the size of our Mississippi, the highest mountains in the world, and climates ranging from arctic Siberia to the near tropical south. Any way you view China's huge geography, it cries out for dams, roads, and urbanization on a scale never before seen in world history.

Keystone of World Economics

New China isn't just a big country with the biggest economy. It's also the fastest growing. Thanks to the economic wisdom of Deng Xiaoping, the pragmatic "free market" Marxist who taught Communists that "being rich is glorious," China's gross national product is expected to grow over six times larger by 2020!

According to economic forecasters, at the current rate of growth it will soon dwarf every other economy in the world — including the USA. Long before 2020, America will be showing up as a very, very poor second to China.

In fact, China is universally seen as the keystone to what will then be the top five economies in the world. Ironically, all five are Pacific Rim trading partners of China. They include the USA, Japan, India, and Indonesia. (The European Union, former Soviet Union, and the oil-rich Middle Eastern countries don't even make the list!)

A Wake-up Call to Americans

For the United States, the message appears to be quite simple: "Move over," and "meet your new rival — the globe's newest superpower!"

Coming to grips with the Chinese challenge is probably the greatest foreign policy crisis for Europe and the United States today. American leaders, both political and spiritual, seem paralyzed in the face of China's explosive new presence on our western horizon.

"America is badly in need of an Asian wake-up call," insists futurist John Nesbitt, author of *Megatrends Asia: Eight Asian Megatrends That Are Reshaping Our World* (Simon & Shuster, New York, 1996). "What is happening in Asia is by far the most important economic trend in the world today. Nothing else comes close, not only for Asians, but also the entire planet."

What's Behind China's Economic Miracle?

The economic renaissance now going on in China (and throughout Asia) boggles the mind. Nesbitt says the raging economic growth in China is fueled by at least seven factors.

(1) BANKING AND INVESTMENT SHIFTS — The so-called "smart money" is now migrating out of the stagnant U.S. economy and onward to Asia, just as it shifted into the United States from Europe in the 19th and 20th centuries. A survey by *Institutional Investor* shows that international business is right now shopping for spots to put $9 trillion more into Asian investments!

(2) FAST GROWTH — Asian economies are returning more than double the world average on investments as industrialization and population continue to grow. Most Asian GNP's are growing at 6 to 10 percent

annually. China is growing in the double digits, five to six times faster than the United States! (The U.S. GNP is growing at a mere 1 - 2 percent annually.)

(3) NEW MIDDLE CLASS — The world's biggest urban middle class is emerging in Asia, while America's middle class is shrinking. In China alone, 120 million peasants have migrated to industrial cities over the last decade. At least 16 of the world's 25 largest cities will soon be in Asia. These newly urbanized populations are huge consumers with growing discretionary incomes.

(4) STRONG FAMILIES WITHOUT WELFARE — Despite the powerful forces doing everything possible to destroy it, the break-up of the Chinese "extended family" system is still culturally unthinkable. The savings rate in most Asian cultures is about 30 percent, precisely because family self-sufficiency still rules. This secret strength contributes to the profitability of Asian business. China does not yet have to tax and weaken business in order to pay for government welfare to prop up broken and dysfunctional families. What's more, it probably will never have this burden. Ironically, the communist government of China provides far less social services to its population than the capitalist "welfare state" of the USA!

(5) STATE OF THE ART TECHNOLOGY — Building to 21st century standards, new manufacturing plants, telecommunications, travel, and data-processing support infrastructure are coming on-line daily. Asia's industrial capacity is already number one in the world. Our high American standard of living is only possible because we import so many cheap consumer goods from China.

(6) CHEAP LABOR — Chinese labor costs are among the lowest on the planet. Most urban Chinese factory laborers earn less than $3 a day! The national average is even lower — and farmers earn as little as 80 cents a day in the countryside! No wonder so many American manufacturers are assembling and producing U.S. consumer goods offshore!

(7) INTER-ASIAN TRADE — Inter-Asian trade already exceeds $500 billion annually, and is greater than Asia's total trade with the rest of the world! This new regional integration is turning the Pacific Rim into a coherent market that is more self-sufficient and therefore will be even more competitive in the next century.

Dawn of the Pacific Century

The bottom line of these trends is simply this: secular experts in every field expect the China/Pacific Rim to become the economically dominant region of the world very early in the 21st century.

After 500 years of humiliating colonization and rule by the Western powers, Asian nations are creating their own political rules in determining the outcome of the game. Marxist and similar secular-humanist political philosophies are still firmly in control of strong central governments. Totalitarian regimes are still common. Democratic freedoms and human rights are willingly sacrificed to satisfy the new greed for wealth.

Fast-paced modernization is extending to military forces as well. Along with growing Chinese prosperity, new communication, education, industrialization, and transportation infrastructures are available to re-arm China. Modernization of the Red Army (PLA) is a top priority.

Unless there is divine intervention on biblical proportions, the 21st century is going to truly be the "Asian Century." The overseas Chinese "Diaspora" largely controls international trade in Pacific Rim capitols. China's new "Lords of the Rim" have established large trading colonies which now control the economies of such port cities as Bangkok, Hong Kong, Manila, Ho Chi Minh, Singapore, Taipei, and Vancouver. In West Coast cities like San Francisco and Los Angeles, Asian "minorities" are the economic engines of local U.S. economies.

And Chinese influence is going far beyond economics. Asian cultures are still driven by powerful spiritual forces. They adapt very slowly and prefer to conquer rather than compromise! Chinese immigrants are bringing with them art, cuisine, iconography, idolatry, language, martial arts, media, medicine, music, science, philosophy, and religion.

While all traditional oriental religions — which spread from Babylon to China on the silk routes — are currently being persecuted in China, they are reviving in the West as New Age cults. Demons long resident in Chinese cultural institutions are often joined to the new Chinese immigration. As a result, we are seeing an export of animism, idolatry, superstition, and paganism to the West.

U.S./China Relations: an Unholy Alliance

Since President Nixon and Henry Kissinger recognized Red China in the Shanghai Accords, the United States and China have floundered along from one crisis to another, trying unsuccessfully to discover a working relationship.

Unfortunately, the only thing that has held the two nations together is an unholy alliance: mutual greed and unrestrained materialism. Social tragedies unthinkable at home are bought and paid for by U.S. interests in China — everything from child labor, slave labor, and cannibalism of fetal tissue and organs.

The State Department and presidents from Ford to Clinton have been unwilling to challenge America's "paper tiger" image in China. Our politicians and economists are hooked on cheap Chinese goods for the United States, and growing technology sales to the Chinese military-industrial complex. Nothing they do seems to be able to reign in Beijing's scorn for our principles of religious freedom and human rights.

This failed American policy of "strategic engagement" with China has sought to use trade to promote justice, freedom, peace, and understanding. So far it has had no apparent effect on the persecution of Chinese Christians or political dissidents.

Our Deadly Misunderstanding

The American government and news media have cultivated a fatal misunderstanding about modern Chinese politics. Chinese communism is not dead or dying. Far from it. Communism in China is vibrant, growing, and stronger than ever. That's because there is something behind it much bigger than communism.

Chinese communism was co-opted at the beginning by the great dragon of Revelation 12:13-17. Satan uses it as a force to resist the Lord, to destroy the bride of Christ in China, and to exploit cultural fears. This has brought bondage, isolation, and death to millions.

The beast is also using Marxism and the Red Army

as a front to rebuild the Chinese military. This is critical as preparations for the Armageddon world war draw closer and closer.

Neo-communism is vibrant and has survived in China because Chairman Mao Tse Tung developed a home-grown variation of secular humanism that appears to be indigenous. In fact, we know now that it was not enslaved to Russian socialism, and did not collapse when European communism fell from power in 1991.

Nor has it remained economically pure Marxism. The Chinese are the natural capitalists of Revelation 18, the merchants of Babylon who have grown rich by trade. Their economic pragmatism and talent for international business inevitably overcomes the British-born socialism of Karl Marx.

No Time for "Commie Bashing"

Today, in fact, modern Chinese communism resembles fascism far more than socialism — with corporate businesses owned by the Red Army, local governments, and national monopolies. These corporations are all operated by Communist party members — the new mandarins of China's "worker-owned state enterprises." This is no time for American Christians to engage in "Commie bashing" or "Red baiting." Far from dead, a new kind of communism rules China today — and dealing with the Chinese government means one must deal with the Communist Party of China (CPC).

Looking back now, it is easy to see that Chinese communism could never have been ideologically pure. Even Mao knew it was impossible, and that's why he tried one last time to cleanse it with the Cultural Revolution.

The Communist Party of China was never successfully controlled by the Moscow-based international communism of her Russian allies. Instead, communism was controlled by an older spiritual force which never released his grip on the Han. He simply changed into the politically correct costume of the 20th century.

China Needs A Spiritual Approach

This basic spiritual misunderstanding was fatal to America's secular policymakers during most of the Korean and Vietnam Wars. It prevented American political and military leaders from using the minimum force needed to stop the Vietnam War. Had the Americans really comprehended the true nature of Chinese communism, the Vietnam War would have ended earlier with a much smaller cost in human lives and destruction.

It also caused the United States to embark on a costly "ring of fire" policy to contain Chinese communism. This deeply flawed U.S. cold war strategy wrongly colored the whole U.S. approach to China — and helped foster the terrorist wars of liberation China sponsored during the 1950s and 60s. It continues to be imbedded in much American thinking today — and will bring failure to anyone who doesn't approach China from a spiritual perspective. We, as Christians, need to make sure we understand what's really happening in China today.

Understanding Chinese Communism

The Bible contains the keys to this understanding of China. We see what's behind Chinese communism for what it really is: a mere mask for territorial spirits under the command of the great dragon, that old serpent, the Antichrist.

Only demon influence can explain the fits of crazed nationalism and irrational xenophobia in modern China — the anti-foreign hatred that has crippled China's ability to form normal relationships with the outside world for five millennia.

By this, I don't mean that China's human rulers are not responsible for their decisions. We all face the coming judgment, including political leaders who have allowed themselves to be influenced by the dragon or demon powers.

Chinese Communism as Reaction to History

However, it is easier to grasp the 20th century Communist takeover of China by understanding its marriage to deeply demonic anti-Christian and anti-foreign roots in the Chinese psyche.

While the historical worship of the Jehovah God can be traced in China from the Zhou Dynasty (1056-256 B.C.), and Christian worship from 635 onward, the local Church in China did not become highly visible until the 19th century. That was when foreign Christian missions entered China on the coattails of British (and other Western) imperialism. As gunboats opened "treaty ports" for American and European traders, the missionaries were never far behind. This legacy is part of the bad image of the Church and Christians in China today.

Robert Morrison of the London Missionary Society, who pioneered translation work on the Chinese Bible, came as a "tentmaking missionary" with the British East India Company in 1807. Later, his firm helped provoke the humiliating Opium Wars (1839-42

and 1858) which led to the Treaties of Nanjing and
Tianjin.

As a result, English drug dealers were able to
legally import narcotics to China from their Burmese
and Indian colonies. These brought very negative social
consequences to China: drug addiction, opium dens,
and crime.

Britain also gained Hong Kong as a colony and free
access to the ports of Fuzhou, Guangzhou, Ningbo,
Shanghai, and Xiamen. Eventually, inland China was
opened to free travel. A special "toleration clause" in the
Treaty of Tianjin permitted missionaries to travel everywhere and preach Christ.

This disgraceful and humiliating trespass was never
forgotten or forgiven by Chinese nationalists. Racist
hate-mongers have portrayed Christians as cultural
imperialists ever since. Ignoring the long history of
Chinese Christianity, the bigots sloganized that "Every
convert to Christ is a son lost to China".

Although Christian missionaries had nothing directly to do with the military actions of their secular
governments, the name of Christ has been popularly
linked to foreign imperialism ever since. Propagandists
have successfully used this sad footnote on history as a
club to beat all Christians.

Chinese believers suffered the most. In the 20th
century, millions have died as martyrs starting from the
1905 Boxer Rebellion right up to the present day. Not
since all foreign ties with western denominations and
cults were cut in 1949 have Chinese leaders started to
doubt their own propaganda.

Far from imperialistic, Chinese Christianity is just
as indigenous to China as Buddhism, Confucianism, or

any of the other religious movements and philosophies that are woven into Chinese culture.

Five decades of persecution, torture, and murder by the Public Security Bureau police have been unable to close down the local churches of China. (The PSB is China's version of the KGB.)

20th Century Worship of Science

Ironically, it was apostate Christian university professors who introduced Marxism, secular humanism, and the worship of science to modern China. Darwinian evolution took on cult-like status and a euphoric optimism swept the country. British atheists taught young students that China didn't need religion, gods, or superstition — including the Lord Jesus Christ.

On May 4, 1919, angry Beijing students protested against the injustices to China in the Treaty of Versailles. This led intellectuals to form the "New Culture movement" which taught that only modern science and democracy could save China from Japanese and other foreign imperialism.

The movement quickly denounced all Chinese traditional religion as superstition. Christianity was lumped in with all other religions at first. However, thanks to Russian influences, Christianity came under particular criticism as an arm of Western imperialism.

Karl Marx, who many feel was a Satan worshipper, provided Chinese students with an appealing intellectual basis for reinforcing atheism and materialism.

When youthful delegates from the movement returned from "Lenin's Moscow Conference for Far Eastern Roilers" in 1922, the attacks on Christians increased. Peace-loving Chinese pastors made easily available victims for the teenage bullies. The World Student Christian Federation conference at Qinghua University was mobbed in March, and an anti-Christian frenzy was released.

Soon it spread throughout all China as the Kuomintang nationalists and the Chinese Communist party formed an alliance to drive out Christian missions. Church buildings, schools, and hospitals were trashed, and Chinese pastors were paraded through the streets for the first time in dunce caps.

Although these early anti-Church campaigns died out in 1927, anti-Christian ideology became frozen into Chinese Communist doctrine. It has continued until the present day. Despite the overwhelming goodness of patriotic Chinese believers — and the benefits Chinese Christians have brought to their society — hardliners have continued to misunderstand and persecute the growing local churches.

Why Hardliners Seem to Hate Christians

Students of Christian history are not at all surprised by hardline Communist attacks on the Church. The current wave of persecution in China is similar to what young Christian congregations have always faced in hostile cultures.

The early church in Europe began with a blood bath similar to what is going on in China today. For nearly 400 years, Jewish and then Roman authorities forced the first Christians to worship illegally and underground. Wave after wave of bloody torture and persecution continued until A.D. 370 when the pendulum swung the other way, and the Church was finally legalized. China is still in this persecution stage.

In my travels throughout China to research this book, I have interviewed dozens of local Chinese pastors. Yet never have I met a bitter or hateful Chinese Christian leader! Even those who survived decades in prison are gentle and forgiving. They speak of the Communists with a compassion we need here in the west. I hope nothing in this book appears as if I'm sowing seeds of anti-Communist hatred.

Many Chinese rejoice at the opportunity to suffer for Christ and gladly tell of their beatings and interrogations by the PSB. Why is this? It is because the Chinese leaders know the truth about their persecutors.

The fact is that the Communists are puppets of a greater power. Paul writes that "we do not wrestle against flesh and blood, but against principalities, against powers, against the rulers of the darkness of this age, against spiritual hosts of wickedness in the heavenly places" (Eph. 6:12).

The Communists themselves don't understand the spiritual force that is causing them to attack the Church in China. That's why the Lord Jesus, when he was being crucified, prayed that God would forgive his killers because "they do not know what they do" (Luke 23:24).

Stephen, the first deacon to be martyred for Christ and the Church, also prayed for his killers, "Lord, do not charge them with this sin" (Acts 7:60).

Chinese missionaries, Stephen, and our Lord all knew that Satan was the real force behind their suffering. The Han people and the territory of China has been claimed and controlled by the great dragon-spirit of the Antichrist, and it is he who is lashing out at us.

Just as the dragon stood before the woman as she gave birth in Revelation 12:4, "to devour her Child as soon as it was born" so he continues to "make war on the rest of her offspring" (Rev. 12:17).

Those who "keep the commandments of God and have the testimony of Jesus Christ" are his prime victims in China today. Satan wants to kill the infant Church now while it is being born. He uses bloody violence whenever it works. He wants to keep his control of China as long as he possibly can because China is a great treasure house to him.

It was Babylon's source of riches in ancient times and it remains a great source of wealth to Babylon the Great and Mystery Babylon today.

The Bible says that Babylon is a habitation of demons, a prison for every foul spirit, and a cage for every unclean and hated bird. In her environs will be found the blood of prophets and saints, of all who are being slain on this earth. This is the real source of our persecution, not the Communist hardliners.

No wonder the dragon holds so tightly onto China. No wonder his legions of demons have become so expert at exploiting the fears, iniquities, and passions of the Han and other Chinese people-groups.

Christians understand that Chinese communism is much more than just another political system. It is a very comfortable camouflage for something deeper and more sinister — a murderous mechanism to destroy the bride of Christ in China. It needs to be understood in its full spiritual dimension — that China today has become one of the greatest strongholds of the Antichrist. It is his last superpower — not just the last superpower of Revelation.

Yet God has already judged Satan. He has declared China free. The time has come to execute the judgment of God upon the great dragon. God has promised to call out a people for His name from every nation. That is the drama that is being played out with such bloody fury in China today.

Mao was right about one thing. The sky is red. But it is red with the blood of Christ and His church. This blood was shed and is still being shed to free the Chinese people from their sins.

In the days ahead, the news media will be filled with many stories about China and the Pacific Rim nations. We can respond in fear and hatred or love and understanding. In this book, I'm asking you to respond as the Chinese Christians do, with patient prayer and charity for those who persecute them.

Chapter 2

Antichrist and the Red Dragon

> *Now the serpent was more subtil than any beast of the field which the Lord God had made* (Gen. 3:1).

The Bible has not left us clueless about the territorial spirit that has headquartered in the Orient for nearly 4,000 years. When you compare Scripture with Scripture, there's no longer any doubt about his awful identity. The true, satanic regent of China has been unmasked at last!

When you come to realize who is really behind the headlines, it starts to make sense. Our spiritual enemy in China is not just the Communists . . . nor a particular person . . . but a supernatural being. We need not fear the future because God has given us victory over the beast — but we dare not underestimate his power, either.

This spirit commands legions of frenzied demons

— the biggest demon armies on earth. Day and night they toil relentlessly to keep the four Chinese races and 55 ethnic minorities in spiritual darkness. He and his demon cohorts slipped a hood over the eyes of the Chinese long before the coming of Christ. They used certain aspects of my beloved as engines of spiritual darkness — and they established spiritual strongholds in the thinking patterns of Chinese families. These patterns of sin and shame have been passed down for centuries.

Satan has ruthlessly resisted many efforts of Christians to remove the spiritual blinders on the Cantonese, Han, Hunanese, and Mandarin nations. His evil host is determined to keep Chinese people bound and gagged until the last possible moment in history.

Why the Dragon Needs China

His Chinese slaves are valuable to him. Coveted. Important. There are two big reasons for Satan to hold onto China: logistics and security. Control of China gives this mastermind of evil immense resources — both human and material. This is an immediate strategic advantage for the end times. China not only controls Asia but has immense influence around the world through overseas "Chinatowns" strategically placed in nearly every major city and country of the world.

China is now "reverse-colonizing" the West through culture and trade! Even the Muslim and Hindu nations of Asia welcome these overseas Chinese trading colonies. The Chinese ghettos of New York, San Francisco, and Toronto are being duplicated everywhere.

I'm not saying all Chinese neighborhoods are haunts for the dragon's demon hordes — or even demon colonies. There are many fine Christians living in

Chinatowns. Usually the crime rates are lower in Chinatowns than other inner cities. However, demon spirits long to possess bodies, and certain families of demons have attached themselves to the Chinese — just as they have to every nation and race. (This is not an argument for racism or prejudice against any race or people, just a spiritual fact of life that helps explain one of the causes for the sin of racism.)

More important to Satan than the overseas Chinese, of course, is his hold on the so-called "Middle Kingdom." This territory has remained a relative safe haven from spiritual attack by Christians. Until recently, it gave him temporary security from the advancing power of the kingdom of God. Now, even in China itself, the territory he controls is shrinking daily.

While the rest of the world was gradually being penetrated by the kingdom of God, China remained isolated. It has served well as the earthly heartland of spiritual Babylon for at least the last 2,000 years — a place where the Gospel light has rarely penetrated. So China has, in effect, been his final fortress against God. Even though much of his Chinese lair is now in ruins, it still remains a formidable defense against the Church.

Remember, Screwtape still holds more souls captive in China than anywhere else on earth. It is the heart of Asia, the most unevangelized continent. It is also his biggest storehouse of both nuclear and conventional weapons. From there, the evil one will launch the biggest expeditionary armies of all history! When China mobilizes to attack the Middle East, more death and destruction will come from Beijing than all the combined wars of the 20th century!

The Demonization of China

Isaiah the prophet seemed to understand that Satan had captured the hearts and minds of the Orient over 3,000 years ago. He cried out, calling Israel to repent, "Because they are filled with eastern ways" (Isa. 2:6).

In fact, archaeologists have found evidence of human sacrifice in China going back to the dawn of Chinese civilization, 5,000 years ago. From the very beginning, China seems to have harbored a murderous demon.

Of course, even before God separated out Israel to be a nation of priests at Jerusalem, Antichrist had developed a religious counter-culture at Babylon — a caravan stop on the way to China and India. Satanic messengers from Babylon obviously found the many indigenous populations of China and India eager to receive Lucifer's counterfeit religious offerings:

(1) IDOLATRY — Antichrist and his demons fueled these flames, animating millions of idols. Idolatry is the first sin. Then and now, it is the basis of all Chinese religion. Idol shelves are found everywhere from kitchen shelves to auto dashboards. Spirit shrines are worshiped only inches away from computer keyboards in the modern, air-conditioned office towers of new China. Despite 50 years of anti-religious indoctrination by the Communist cadre, the largest Buddha images in the world are still being built and worshiped in China. Even Mao, the scientific atheist founder of China's Communist party has been idolized. His image is now being made into temple-gods, and an entire temple has been built to worship him in his native village!

(2) MAMMON — Christ warned clearly that you

cannot serve God and Mammon. Antichrist found, along the silk roads to China, a commercial, industrious people — a nation totally caught up with the "here and now" concerns of daily living. Covetousness, gluttony, and greed still motivate most of the China traders and their foreign partners. Paul described such "wealth worshipers" as men whose god is their belly. Chinese culture worships money and the power it brings.

(3) MOLECH — Cannibalism and human sacrifice are nothing new in China. Infanticide and abortion have been practiced since the beginning of history. Recent reports that human organs and aborted babies are being "harvested" and sold for "health purposes" come as no surprise. Words like "medical science" and "medical research" are used to cover the truth of this grisly business — but it is nothing less than murder and cannibalism of the innocent.

The spirit of the same god whose white-hot idol arms received child sacrifices in Babylon and Israel is alive in China today.

(4) ASHTEROTH, THE BLACK ARTS, AND SORCERY — Chinese folk religion thrives on astrology, divination, fortune telling, geometricy, luck, spiritualism, and a thousand other curious arts. While 50 years of secular humanism has sought to "modernize" China, the popular reliance on magic runs deeply through everyday life.

Socialism struggles vainly to eliminate the stubborn springs of animism and superstition that still water frightened souls all across Asia. In nearby Japan, which chose to modernize through Western science and technology 100 years before China, Shinto folk festivals still regularly bring a modern, industrial nation to a complete halt. Millions climb mountains to bow before trees and rocks inhabited by particular demon spirits.

BBC broadcaster Alasdair Clayre summed it up well when he quoted a missionary saying "In China the educated believe nothing and the uneducated believe everything."[1] The imaginations of the Chinese are populated by a vast pantheon of gods and goddesses, fairies and ghosts. These spirits inhabit particular lakes, mountains, and woodlands within walking distance of every department store, library, laboratory, and missile silo.

Yet, over all these spirits is one spirit more evil than all the others — a spirit ruler well-known to Bible students. For the time being, let's just call him the "evil genius of the 10/40 window."

Who Is This Evil Genius?

The true identity of this ruling entity — the spirit almost universally idolized as a dragon or snake — is finally clear. When you realize who he is, you suddenly understand why controlling the wealth and population of China is so essential to his ultimate plans for planet earth. Without China, he cannot accomplish his final act of suicidal madness.

You have to understand that China is only a steppingstone for this dark prince. The dragon really doesn't want the Chinese people or care about them for what they are. That would be love. No, China is merely a springboard for him — a springboard to world dominion. The dragon is about to reveal himself to the whole world — and already has to many prophets of the New World Order. Most Christian scholars believe he will actually achieve his global ambitions, during the seven terrible years of the Great Tribulation.

John Hagee in his bestseller, *Beginning of the End*, believes that even China will eventually turn against him. But it will be too late to stop the death and destruction by then. The doom of 200 million Oriental soldiers will be sealed. (Since the dragon desires to send as many Americans and Chinese to hell as possible, he wins even when he loses!)

Right now, this malignant architect of Armageddon chooses to remain discreetly out of sight. At least most of the time. As we write, he is wrapped in a Marxist disguise. But his identity is more and more obvious as history unfolds.

Compromised Camouflage

The fact is, this demon who sometimes calls himself "Big Snake" can't keep his awful secret! Try as he might, he is rather inconsistent in disguising his identity. He is so vain. He often tips his hand just to show off. This guy has an insane ego problem. While created to be one of the most invisible creatures on earth, he uses his skills now to hide and deceive. However, even he can only keep the "big lie" up for just so long!

He most often slips during idolatrous worship. That's when he just can't help revealing his identity to devoted followers. He loves to receive worship intended for the true God and receive it unto himself. Thus the Chinese public sees his image in almost every temple. Throughout Asia, the dragon is a favorite theme for demon-possessed artisans, painters, and mystics who have seen him. They in turn reproduce his image in art.

The dragon loves to show off his icon everywhere he can — from jailhouse tattoos to temple walls; from emperor's robes to the Victory Column near the main gate of the Forbidden City of Beijing. He will not rest, in fact, until his idol image is actually set up in Jerusalem (see Rev. 13:15). Lately, western graphic artists have enjoyed portraying him on book jackets, magazine covers, and cartoons.

A Satanic Systems Engineer

This spirit is also a master dis-organizer, a kind of spiritual "systems engineer." He is a devisor of flawed schemes to control financial affairs, religious freedom, and peace. He just can't help it! That's why everywhere he goes there is famine, miscarriages of justice, oppression, poverty, and war — just the opposite of what he skillfully promises. Can this guy lie? You bet. Every election, he makes countless promises he can never keep.

Warmonger to the world, older Christians have seen him foment two huge world wars in the 20th century! Baby boomers have seen his long, claw-like tentacles reach out as far as Afghanistan, Bosnia, Cambodia, Indonesia, Philippines, Sudan, and Vietnam. Always promising economic progress, justice, and peace, this murderous spirit produces massacres instead — usually in the name of some religion or ideology. (He doesn't care which!) The fact is that death comes whenever he gets even a small foothold. And millions die wherever he gets a firm enough grip to extend his reign of terror.

That's why China has had 5,000 years of schemes like the Great Leap Forward (famine), the Great Cultural Revolution (reign of terror), and the One Child Policy (massacre).

Just look at what we've seen in the two decades in

Asia alone. Over 20 years of civil war in Afghanistan have left millions dead and the terror still grinds forward in Kabul; 2-3 million were massacred by his Khmer Rouge agents in Cambodia; 2 million Chinese died in Indonesia after the Suharto failed coup in 1967; 150,000 Christians have died at the hands of Muslim separatists in the Philippines from 1976 to 1996; and 3 million died in the Vietnamese civil war. In China the death toll must now be 100 million or more. Plus, don't forget the wars and terrorism in Bangladesh, India, Laos, Sri Lanka, and Tibet. All this carnage has occurred, says the Bible, in a time when he is being "restrained" (2 Thes. 2:6). Just imagine what it will be like when he is released!

The Great Dragon's China Plan Bible students will have already guessed his identity. The Great Dragon that has ruled China for 3,000 years is none other than the anti-Christ spirit of Lucifer himself. Antichrist is one part of the *unholy* trinity of evil that mocks and imitates the Holy Trinity of God. This "big snake" will eventually animate and empower the end-times Antichrist of Revelation 13:4 — a man possessed by Satan himself. He is the very same lying spirit that successfully deceived Eve in the Garden of Eden.

Soon, he will possess his final human form. An enormously popular man, he is only known to us in the Bible by his code name, the Antichrist. He is coming soon — many believe he has already been born. Meanwhile, his spirit already lives in the earth and has possessed a long series of petty tyrants like Genghis Khan, Hitler, and probably a host of anonymous colonels. This, I remind you, does not mean these evil rulers are free of guilt, because Antichrist only possesses yielded vessels.

The Bible tells us a whole lot about the New World Order he is now establishing. We can also learn a lot about him by studying the lands which have been cursed with his long, direct rule.

In fact, this spirit has reigned almost unopposed in countries like China, Iran, and Iraq since time began. The Bible calls him the Prince of Persia (Dan. 10:20) and the Persian Empire has snaked its way all across Asia. Missions experts have defined the territory he clings to as the "10/40 Window" — an expanse from the Sea of Japan to West Africa, from 10 degrees to 40 degrees longitude.

Over this area looms a dark cloud, a thunderstorm of evil. It seeks vainly to insert itself between God and man. Under that cloud is the epicenter of all the world's misery. Most of the world's disease, hatred, oppression, poverty, violence, and war come from the 10/40 window. In the very heart of this spiritual darkness is China — and God is today shooting laser beams of light right through that darkness. No wonder the cloud is lifting in places.

This cloud is the spirit of Antichrist. A force. A personality. A fallen angel. And soon to be a human being. Yet, Christ is the light of the world and His gospel breaks through that cloud, just as a tiny candle lights the darkest room.

Questions That Demand Answers

Whether you are a believer or not, whether you are American or Chinese — there are questions about this coming "man of sin" that demand answers. How and when did Antichrist come to rule China in the fist place? How long will he continue to rule? What can we learn from his behavior that will affect us and our families?

Why is his totalitarian grip on China slipping? Why is he reaching out to control or destroy the USA next? What could that mean for Europe, the Middle East, and the rest of the world community? Why is he exporting his terror tactics? What is the nature of his warfare against you?

These are the kinds of strategic questions we will try to answer in the remaining chapters of this book. If you're a Christian, you need to know how saints are to respond and storm the gates of his dark kingdom! First, how do we know the Red Dragon of China is the same dragon as Antichrist in the Bible.

Is the Red Dragon Really Antichrist?

Which territorial spirit controls China? How can we be sure that it really is Antichrist? Police hunt criminals by identifying an "M.O." (or "Modus Operandi"). When they find the way a lawbreaker operates, it is easier to track and identify who he is. The Bible describes Antichrist as "lawless" in 2 Thessalonians 2:3-12 and gives us his M.O. in several books of the Bible. These six characteristics of Antichrist are his fingerprints. We will always find one or more at the scene of his crimes.

When you find one of these prints, look for the others. Then check to see if they match the fingerprints of China's dragon prince.

"So what?" asks the skeptical unbeliever. "Even if the Dragon is really Antichrist, why should we care? Is it really that important that we know who we're dealing with in Beijing?"

Obviously from the Bible, the answer is "yes!"

God gave us a clear picture of Antichrist for a good reason. He wants us to know how to spot the man of sin. That's the only way to protect ourselves, our families, our nation, and our church groups. Knowing our enemy helps us develop tactics to spiritually counterattack.

If the Red Dragon really is Antichrist, then we know how to defeat him. Knowing that he is supernatural helps us understand that we can never have victory over him in the natural. The weapons of our warfare are not carnal but supernatural (2 Cor. 10:4). Atomic bombs, boycotts, diplomacy, trade agreements, treaties, the Navy, and trade wars will not defeat him. The Bible begs us not to trust these human instruments to contain him (see Job 41). I'm not saying that human strength and wisdom are not sometimes a gift from God. They are, but we are forbidden to trust in them. Our attack is to be primarily spiritual warfare — and if you're not comfortable with that, then get some prayer warriors on your team who are true believers.

The nation or president that seeks to defeat Antichrist economically, politically, or militarily will fail. That's why the recent American presidents — particularly Presidents Reagan, Bush, and Clinton have failed to restrain the Red Dragon. The Christian who seeks to fight personal battles in his own strength will fail, too. The great dragon leviathan will be defeated only by the Lord in the spiritual realm (Isa. 27:1).

Six Antichrist Behavior Patterns

That's why it is so vital that you know the six sure ways you can spot anti-Christ activity. When you do, you can begin to fight primarily in the spiritual realm rather than the earthly. These tests apply to his actions in governments, institutions, families, or individuals.

First, Antichrist deceives the world. Nothing reveals Antichrist better than his supernatural ability to deceive the world — he is the greatest con artist of all time. He is called "one and many" because of his ability to don a thousand disguises (1 John 2:18). John portrays Antichrist as a false teacher (2 John 7-11) whose web of lies can only be resisted by dis-fellowship!

Separation is not popular today in this age of ecumenism and global thinking. Antichrist is moving society toward one religion, one economy, one world government, and one global military. However, "holiness unto the Lord" is still the motto of God's people.

That's why we're told to not even greet Antichrist or entertain his ambassadors as guests. He is such a fantastic liar that he can, for a time, fool the saints (Matt. 24:24). That makes him the most dangerous "friend" of all. Using art, media, linguistics, music, and philosophy, he has no conscience about rewriting history or redefining theology. The facts or truth are irrelevant to him, except as prelude to a lie. Often, he appears at first like one of your own family members. He seeks to infiltrate every institution, even Christian church groups.

Once inside, he patiently waits — baiting his victims with half-truths. He is a master of "double-speak" — he calls evil good. He adapts. He pretends.

Antichrist is like a mole. Espionage agencies plant moles in other governments and agencies. They have to seem helpful and part of the program until the moment comes for them to strike. Antichrist works this way, even in Christian organizations and churches.

He is skilled at adapting to any church, movement, political party, profession, or communication medium.

He works a "con" or lie for years if necessary to split families, marriages, the Church, or nations. He is the "tares" among the wheat that Jesus told us about in Matthew 13:8. These tares often grow in the highest places of leadership and power.

Second, Antichrist is a false god. He seeks personal worship. He cannot rest until he has it (2 Thess. 2:3-4). Even in atheistic, secular guises like communism or humanism, Antichrist will possess megalomaniacs like Hitler, Lenin, Mao, and Stalin. Such men provide a temporary vehicle for humanity to worship him. Antichrist both uses and hates religion. He uses it when he can be worshiped through it, and he hates it when it worships the true God and rivals his control over people.

He loves to speak soothing words of peace, and has no problem possessing church, judicial, political, or religious leaders if available. Of course, he animates idols of all kinds. He is skilled at manipulating art, icons, images, and statues. This is why idolatry of all kinds has been forbidden by God and all His true prophets from the dawn of time.

Third, Antichrist is a killer who persecutes the Church. Revelation 13:7 says, "It was given to him to make war with the saints and to overcome them" in every tribe, people, tongue, and nation. Antichrist has an evil commission opposite of the Great Commission Christ gave the Church. He is the force behind the persecution of Christians in China — not the Communists. In fact, he is the global force persecuting the Church everywhere. Christ commanded us to go preaching, teaching, and baptizing. He goes about undoing our work with a baptism of fire. In times of tribulation, Antichrist retraces the steps of the missionaries with the sword — killing and destroying believers.

Fourth, Antichrist is a miracle worker. Antichrist performs wonders and signs of all kinds. He loves to mix magic and technology. Most of his wonders are scientifically based, but some are occultic. Many in China — like the Great Wall, the Grand Canal, or the Long March — were accomplished by superhuman courage, dedication, sacrifice, and wisdom. Others are merely slight of hand, psychological manipulation, and propaganda. All are real in some sense of the word. They are designed to appeal to the Chinese psychology. Second Thessalonians 2:9 says he comes with "all power, signs, and lying wonders."

Warlocks, witch doctors, and shamans from thousands of false cults perform healings and imitate the miracles of the Holy Spirit daily. Bloodless surgeons in the Philippines, Chinese martial artists, channelers in Thailand, and the fire-walkers of India all amaze the gullible. It is safe to say that nearly every miracle or movement of the Holy Spirit is sometimes imitated by Antichrist as part of his plan to deceive and lead astray the saints.

Fifth, Antichrist denies that God has a son — all false religion or ideology which denies the deity of Christ is anti-Christ (1 John 2:22, 4:3, and 2 John 7). This is the ultimate litmus test for spotting Antichrist. Any ideology, religion, philosophy, or political movement that denies the true identity of Jesus Christ is definitely part of the Antichrist's worldwide web of lies.

When he has to, Antichrist can specialize in teaching a peculiar doctrine that appears good or at least harmless to Christians. Sometimes it is one side of truth. In fact, he loves to pick up one interpretation or even a particular practice of piety and push it almost to the breaking point. This is how basically innocent denominational traditions become cultic and divisive.

It is often a legitimate practice of piety. Christians are allowed to differ on beliefs such as diet, dress codes, holy days, or other matters of conscience such as unsettled debates about doctrine, prophecy, or theology (see 2 Thess. 2:11). Why does Antichrist fasten onto such petty doctrines?

It's part of his war of attrition. If he can get Christians worn down fighting about petty points of doctrine, he hopes that he can slip "the big one" past us! When testing a spirit, get down right away to his or her position on the deity of Christ.

If someone's teaching on who Christ is does not square with Scripture, separation is your only recourse. This fact is so hard to accept in today's "live and let live" culture of compromise and tolerance. While we are commanded to live in peace with all men, separation from ungodly teachings (as well as unholy lifestyles!) remain essential to our covenant with God.

Sixth, Antichrist is lawless. Paul describes him as "the man of sin" or the "son of perdition" in 2 Thessalonians 2:3 and goes on to call him the "lawless one" (see verse 8). In both the epistles of John and Thessalonians, where Antichrist is described, he is contrasted with the righteousness of true saints. Christ's followers are characterized by love and holiness. Antichrist's followers are hateful and unholy. Antichrist is a malicious pervert, a rebel at heart. He steals and kills for the fun of it. He is of his father, a predator who roams the earth seeking whom he may devour (1 Pet. 5:8).

So we see the Antichrist of Scripture is: (1) deceptive, (2) seeks worship, (3) persecutes the Church, (4) does wonders, (5) denies Christ, and (6) loves sin. Does that describe the dragon we know has controlled Chinese history? Bingo! We have a match.

The Role of Antichrist

This spiritual monster is called many names in the Bible. Among them, "the man of sin" and "son of perdition" (2 Thess. 2:3); "the lawless one" (2 Thess. 2:8); "Antichrist" (1 John 2:18,22); and "the beast" (Rev. 11:7). He is none other than the personification of Satan himself. God had an only Son who is destined to rule this world, the Lord Jesus Christ. Satan tries to imitate this through Antichrists. There have been many throughout history. In fact, scholars and saints through the ages have been convinced that they saw Antichrist in some of the dictators, popes, and tyrants of their age.

However, none of the many Antichrists of history will compare to the final Antichrist in deceptive skills or unbending terror. When "the" Antichrist of Revelation comes, he will be a man totally possessed of Satan — the Devil's "only begotten son!" The exact opposite of Jesus Christ, he will struggle to replace our Lord and rule in his stead. This action provokes the Battle of Armageddon and millions of Chinese will die as a result.

That's why it is important that we don't view the spirit of Antichrist as a fairy tale. Satan wants us to think of Antichrist as mere myth. He wants us to joke about Antichrists and the Antichrist. That's why he chose the dragon disguise. It is terrible, yet attractive, and kind of innocent. In fact, he even portrays the dragon to children as a soft, cuddly playtoy . . . a gentle dinosaur. He would like everyone to think of him as "Puff the Magic Dragon who lives by the sea." (That has to be one of the most satanic songs ever written!)

But the Red Dragon is not a concept, cartoon character, fantasy, joke, lyric, metaphor, symbol, or toy! The Bible teaches us that he is a real person as well as a system (2 Thess. 2:3,7). He is a "shape shifting" demon who has personality characteristics just as you and I do. He possesses personhood as does God the Father, the Holy Spirit, and the Lord Jesus Christ. Antichrist is cunning, vain, and violent — a rebel angel who hates Jesus Christ and His true Church with every bit of his perverted strength.

Why Did the Dragon Choose China?

How and why would such a spirit be attracted to China and the Chinese people? Let's speculate here, based on what we know of Antichrist. He is a cunning, militaristic spirit. The Orient was probably nothing more than a target of opportunity. China was attractive to him in the first place because it had geographical advantages and was undefended.

First of all, it was as far from Israel and Jehovah as one could get on the ancient map. It had a growing population to inhabit — just what the Devil wanted! Satan watched with envy as God chose to "make covenant" and dwell among Abraham's children — to protect, guide, prosper, and make them holy. There was obviously little hope for him there as long as they were "the apple of His eye" and "were inscribed on the palms of His hand." Then he saw God select Jerusalem as an earthly site for His temple dwelling. He hated that. He envied it too — and still envies it today. God was invading "his territory" with love and mercy, establishing a witness of His holiness among men. As long as Almighty God dwelt in the tabernacle and temples of Israel — there was little hope for him to directly possess that land.

On the other hand, God had already scattered the tower builders of Babylon to the ends of the earth. Many had undoubtedly settled in the fertile valleys of the Huang He, Chang Jiang, and Xi Jiang rivers. Here were people groups among whom Satan could establish a rival to Israel. Antichrist could not pass up this opportunity.

I'm not sure that Satan yet fully understood the role that the coming Messiah would play in Jewish history. The Bible says that even the angels in heaven didn't understand it at first. But if he did, he probably started dreaming of beginning a dynasty leading to the birth of a human Antichrist, an "anti-messiah" of his own!

Not surprisingly, from the beginning of Chinese history one finds parallels to Israel. But not the true God. There is temple worship with sacrifices and a host of other "covenant" relationships between the Chinese emperors and the dragon. That imitates the Levitical priesthood of Israel. I'll never forget walking through the Temple of Heaven in Beijing where the emperors were required to make offerings on behalf of the people. In their priestly robes, they were offering to Antichrist what the Levitical priesthood offered to the one true God of Israel. As early as the Tang Dynasty, Emperor Taizone (626-49) is shown with double-dragons embroidered on his vestments. Even the Chinese name for their country ("the Middle Kingdom") hints at Satan's stairway to heaven — their special relationship with

Antichrist's rivalry to the plan of God for our salvation.

Second, the Himalayan Mountains of Tibet and Nepal gave Lucifer the high ground he adores (Isa. 14:13-14). He dwells in high places like the sacred mountain of Taishan in Shandong province. All his false temples are amazingly similar — reaching upward to heaven. Be it at the Tower of Babel, the pyramids of Egypt, the Inca copies of ancient Ziggarots in Mexico, or the stupas of Burma — all exalt the concept of man and demons reaching upward. (It makes one wonder what spirit is behind the modern skyscrapers of Chicago, Shanghai, or Penang — let alone the steeples of medieval cathedrals in Europe!)

It is no surprise that so many forms of animism, demon worship, Hinduism, and Buddhism have been born in the Himalayan Mountains. Nor is it a surprise that the Communists today are so determined to maintain Chinese sovereignty over Tibet. Perversely, the dragon today persecutes the Lamistic Buddhist monks of Tibet which he helped create, just as he smashed ancient idols in the Cultural Revolution. No wonder the Communists are so fearful of rivals. They instinctively know that Antichrist will someday betray them. Communists live in fear, evidence of their tormenting control by Antichrist.

Is it possible that the Tibetan Buddhists are no longer worshiping Antichrist as they once did? Is there a demonic rebellion of sorts in the Himalayas? Maybe it's even more simple. Perhaps it's merely the capricious meanness and jealousy of Antichrist in action! He is far more cruel to his own subjects than he is to Christians. After all, we are protected by God and the holy angels.

Third, Antichrist obviously chose China because it was remote but not inaccessible. King Solomon traded with China. The ancient silk road superhighway went from the New Testament port of Antioch to Changan (Sian). Silk routes also went by sea from Jerusalem to Ningbo in the Tang and Song dynasties. The caravan land routes went through Baghdad and connected with nearly all the ancient capitals from Babylon to Khanbalik (Beijing).

Antichrist needed fast travel for his armies, priests, and trade. He always wants the logistical advantage. Using the silk routes, Antichrist transferred magic, superstition, and false religious ideas across the ancient map — along with military forces and fortunes in trade. Even today one senses Antichrist at work in airports, bus stations, ports, and train depots.

The Rejection of Jewish Light

Where was our loving God while Antichrist was ensnaring the Chinese race? Did God leave China without any light during the pre-Christian era? Probably not. The Magi came from the East to worship Christ at his birth. Chinese and Jewish traders must have shared religious views. Yet Chinese religionists rejected the "One God" of Mount Sinai for more practical "man-centered" religions.

We must remember that no one and no race is separated from God who doesn't choose to be. Once the early Orientals had chosen idols rather than the true God, Antichrist was ever vigilant to protect them from messengers of the living God. He provided clever alternatives and substitutes for the Mosaic Law through religious teachers such as Kong Qui (Confucius), Lao

Zi (Tao), and Sakyamuni (Buddhism).

Yet the Chinese continued to have regular trading contacts with Israel — at least by the time of King Solomon. From a biblical perspective however, the first actual immigrations of Jews to China could not have happened before the Assyrian captivity (722 B.C.). More likely, they first came from the time of Babylonian exile to the Roman Conquest (586 B.C. to A.D. 70). Later, after the Romans expelled the Jews from Jerusalem, they came east in much larger numbers, mostly to Chinese Turkestan along the old Silk Road. Most Chinese scholars agree that the Jews did not arrive in large groups until the Tang and Song dynasties.[2]

Either the Jews of China were very poor witnesses or Kong Qiu did an excellent job of inoculating the Chinese against belief in God. Both were probably true. How much persecution was exerted on the Jews of China we cannot tell. However, some of the Chinese Jews survived well into the Christian era. They all but disappeared during the Communist Revolution — finally assimilated into the dominant culture through spiritual compromise and marriage.

Antichrist Welcomes Religion

For Antichrist to insure the failure of Judaism in China, he welcomed a dizzying array of lying, religious spirits in its place. As God revealed more and more light to the Jews — and finally sent Christ to save the world — Antichrist imported philosophy and dogma tailored to pre-empt certain foundational teachings of God's Word.

Believers in each of these great non-Christian faiths found that they had swallowed a "philosophical" poison pill — one which prevented them from intellectually accepting the good news of God's grace.

Buddhism is a good example of this kind of spiritual sabotage. Antichrist brought Buddhist missionaries from India around the same time the first Christian missionaries arrived in China. Sakyamuni's disciples taught the Chinese that there was no God or hope of salvation. Life took its meaning from its suffering — a kind of well-deserved purgatory on earth that each human earns and therefore brings upon himself. The only hope to escape endless reincarnation was in exercise, meditation, and good works. Through Buddhism, Antichrist taught the Chinese the lie that man controls his own destiny and has no need of a Saviour.

When Buddhism was added to the already popular Confucianism and Taoism, it wrapped the Chinese soul in a three-fold mental cord that was not easily broken. All three doctrines denied the existence of God and centered on ways to find success in the material world by manipulating the spiritual.

Confucianism provided Chinese culture with an ethical and moral hierarchy based on half of the Ten Commandments. This cunning social order has survived centuries of famine and war, but provides no place for personal responsibility or relationship to God.

Taoist mysticism rebels against the imposed order of Confucianism, celebrating both active and passive resistance to God through the worship of creation rather than the creator. It is the pagan "go with the flow" magic of "yin and yang."

These powerful combinations of human religion and worldly power were successful in withstanding some of the early missionaries who came to China. Not understanding the spiritual powers of Antichrist, the early Nestorians attempted to impose religious systems. They disappeared after a few hundred years — compromised by doctrinal error and most likely massacred by Muslim invaders.

Next the Jesuits and other Catholic orders attempted evangelism through catechism or indoctrination. They had short-lived success introducing education, science, and technology. This, too, failed to smash the gates of the spiritual hell that imprisoned the Chinese.

It would not be until the 19th century that God would answer global prayers for doors to open in Chinese hearts. As millions around the world prayed, a supernatural grace was poured out upon the Chinese. The Word of God arrived in China and gradually a remnant put their faith in Christ during almost 100 years of evangelism.

Antichrist Strikes Back

Then Antichrist struck back with Marxism, a modern ideology from Germany that promised the Chinese heaven on earth. Like the earlier religions and superstitions, communism offered the same old bait — material salvation on earth by man's own human effort without God. Chinese political leaders fell for it again. However, this time, Antichrist failed to feed the newly-awakened hunger of China's masses for salvation.

Even Antichrist has not been able to withstand the grace of God and the power of his Holy Spirit that continued into the 20th century. It all began in the 17th and 18th centuries when the Chinese inventions of gunpowder, paper, and moveable type finally reached

Europe. Everything Satan does to rebel against God comes back to haunt and destroy him.

Spiritual Warfare Begins

Soon after, Bibles were printed in the languages of the European masses. By the 19th century, revivals broke out in England and the United States as the gospel was freely preached there for the first time. The love of God began to overwhelm certain simple-minded foreigners with an aching desire to bring the light of salvation to the Chinese:

• Robert Morrison, a student of Chinese, was forbidden to enter China by the emperor. He finally was permitted to stay in 1807 by getting a clerking job for a godless commercial firm the Chinese did allow — the British East India Company. At night, he struggled to translate the Word of God into Chinese and helped produce one of the first Bibles in Chinese.

• Hudson Taylor, a young medical student in England, gave up the promise of a lucrative career to bring the gospel. With these fresh movements of the Holy Spirit came a renewed missionary vision for the Chinese. He was among the first of thousands who would give their lives bringing the gospel to inland China.

• Lottie Moon, a teenage girl in the hills of central Virginia, gave up hopes for marriage and family to help reach the children of China for Christ.

It was not gunboats, education, medicine, or trade that opened the gates of China to these missionaries. That is the human explanation by the Marxists who still call them "foreign devils" — and by unbelieving historians who are doing Antichrist's propaganda work for the 21st century.

No, these 19th century missionaries succeeded only because they brought simple Bible truth and faith to the Chinese for the first time. They overcame Antichrist by the blood of the Lamb and the power of their testimony. Love won out!

Finally, after 50 centuries, Antichrist was dealing with believers who fought him with spiritual warfare using the weapons of Ephesians 6:11-16. As a result, indigenous church and mission movements were finally begun. If you use these methods, you will also win the victory over Antichrist that you need today.

Of course, Antichrist struck back with bloody terrorism, provoking wars and rumors of wars in order to stop the spread of the gospel. Many Chinese died as a result of the Boxer Rebellion, and a long series of other persecutions which continue to this day — but he is waging the losing defense in a war of attrition.

Antichrist on the Defensive

Suddenly in the mid-19th century, Antichrist found that he had to re-focus. In order to hold onto his Asian slaves, he had to disrupt the revival in Europe and the United States. He had to begin false theological and political movements in the West that would corrupt and undermine missions. Among the movements he decided to launch were universalism to destroy Christianity; fascism to destroy the Zionists who were bent on restoring Israel; and communism to destroy freedom.

It wasn't easy on humanity. Before the end of the 20th century, Antichrist would have to use many other horrible events to try to stop the evangelism of China: the Boxer Rebellion, the Japanese imperial invasion, two world wars, the Communist Revolution, and Islamic fundamentalism.

Yet Christianity has not been stopped. Instead, a purer and stronger church is emerging in China — a missionary church that has made evangelism, spiritual warfare, and worship its top priorities. Christians around the world are praying for the persecuted church of China. Chinese believers like me have been dispersed to all the nations of the earth, and we are forming a network that will help complete the final evangelization of Asia in the 21st century.

Antichrist Loosens His Grip

All this spiritual activity inside and outside China has caused Antichrist to loosen his grip in many ways. Since the Communist Revolution, persecution has been intense but broken by periods of relative freedom.

More important probably, has been Antichrist's continued preoccupation with the outside world. In the first half of the century he focused on disrupting the Church and missions in Europe. Then in 1949 the land of Israel was returned to the Jews. Since then, Antichrist has more and more been drawn to re-focus his envy on the temple and the Holy Land. Now he must put together the Anglo-European alliance that will support his take-over of the world's economy, military, and religion.

So his seemingly powerful grip on China since 1949 has not been all that it appears. It is really a death grip — not the grip of a powerful spirit in confident control. As much as Antichrist wants to continue oppressing the growing Church in China, he is going to have to release it more often and for longer periods of time.

You see, the dragon Antichrist is finite. His forces are limited. And now they are spread out as never before. He cannot hold China as tightly — or any territory for that matter. He is reaching out for the world. His attention is more focused on his new world capital in Jerusalem, and in what he has to do to deceive the nations of Europe and the USA.

Watch for Antichrist to be more dramatic, creative, and violent than ever. Now he must take bigger, bolder, more desperate steps. Will you be ready when his agents come to your business, home, or school? Antichrist is no longer limiting his warfare to China and the 10/40 window. He is on the move everywhere.

[1]Alasdair Clayre, *The Heart of the Dragon* (Boston, MA: Houghton Mifflin, 1985), p. 51.

[2]Sidney Shapiro, *Jews in Old China* (New York, NY: Hippocrene Books, 1984), p.187.

Chapter 3

Armies for Armageddon

And the sixth angel poured out his vial upon the great river Euphrates; and the water thereof was dried up, that the way of the kings of the east might be prepared (Rev. 16:12).

Of all the sad and terrible chapters that have to be written in the blood of Chinese history, this is the saddest. Especially for me as a Chinese-American believer.

For our people, whose primary corporate instinct is survival, China's coming tribulation is horror beyond imagination. It will be the holocaust of all holocausts. No act of God, no war, no natural disaster, no plague, no action of any dictator, has ever taken so many lives so quickly.

China has spent nearly 5,000 years successfully

preparing for earthquakes, floods, famines, plague, and war. No race has developed such a fine-honed sense of collective preparation and survival.

Yet, in this catastrophe, hundreds of millions of Chinese will die horrible, violent deaths — both civilians and military. In a brief period, less than seven years, three times the population of the United States will be wiped off the face of the earth!

A People Prepared for Slaughter

Perhaps no people-group but the Chinese are prepared to make such a sacrifice and keep going. Maybe that's why the dragon has chosen us to lead his end-times armies — to be the last superpower. From the time Chinese are babies, everything is subject to the will of the collective good; the family first — and now to the masses and the nation. The gospel, with its call to make a personal decision for Christ and live a life of free moral choices, has never been fairly considered by most Chinese.

Before we get to the place where we are allowed to make a free choice, every shred of individualism has been beaten down. Every idiosyncrasy, every bit of self-expression and even personal privacy are punished in the dragon's lifelong "shame campaign" against personality. Historically, no one is allowed to question the authority of the family, and today that is being replaced by the state. That's why, when the orders for Armageddon are given, I have no doubt that Chinese soldiers will march to their deaths without a murmur.

The fact is, the Bible doesn't just predict the destruction of the Red Army — but all of modern China as we know it. This final world war, and the events surrounding it, will destroy both fish and sea — both the

Chinese infantry and people who support it.

Why Rearm Now?

Even now, no one is questioning the insane drive to re-arm China. It doesn't even make any economic sense for China to arm this huge expeditionary force — let alone military sense. The Chinese are a frugal, life-oriented people who are not prone to wasteful rainbow chasing. That's why it's not even very Chinese to gamble on such a wasteful, unprofitable venture.

Why build the biggest military industrial complex ever? And why build it now? Arming and supporting these millions of troops requires an infrastructure of no real value to Chinese trade or development. So why, after three decades of relative peace, is China relentlessly re-arming? Who is this mysterious "new" enemy that our people are so very afraid to face?

The Bible predicts exactly who this "enemy" is. While China's leaders still don't even know who they're preparing to fight — Antichrist does. It is the Red Dragon who has set China on this suicidal course toward war; a great march toward fiery destruction beyond anyone's imagination.

Profits for U.S. Arms Industry

Meanwhile, we, as Americans, have a very big economic interest in the exploding new Chinese arms industry. Our government and the U.S. economy are the real senior partners in this amazing "arms race" against a still unacknowledged enemy. As I wrote this chapter, a Pentagon spokesman in Washington was asked about the vast amounts of U.S. "surplus" military hardware now appearing in China. He said it wouldn't surprise him, although he couldn't confirm or deny anything, that the United States can't track where all our old weapons end up!

The truth is that to modernize for 21st century warfare, Asia's militarists are dependent upon a massive transfer of American capital, industry, and technology to China. This is what is making it all possible. The dragon is building the world's biggest military industrial complex — thanks to Chinese labor and American engineering.

The U.S. government is working to patch up its tattered relations with China. Our current arms sales to Taiwan and "the little tigers" aren't enough to help balance our trade deficits — but they help. The only way to erase our trade deficit overnight is bigger arms and technology shipments to mainland China.

This is why President Clinton is calling for reduced and eliminated tariffs on the Asian electronic and telecommunications trade. The "information superhighway" must extend to China to carry intelligence, as well as real superhighways that will transport men and material to the front lines.

China's Cover Story

Before we look at what the Bible says about Chinese militarism in the endtimes, let's briefly survey the "cover stories" Beijing gives for the current arms buildup.

There are three main arguments for "modernizing" and equipping the Red Army with "first strike" capacity: (1) fears of external attack, (2) the threat of civil unrest, and (3) unresolved border disputes with neighboring states.

First, what about those "external" threats? Since

China no longer has outside imperialists eyeing her territory, this is the hardest rationale to develop! Yet the same demon spirit that possessed Qin Shihuangdi to build the 4,160 mile-long Great Wall is now building another wall. The Great Wall was built using bricks, mortar, and slave labor. Hundreds of thousands, perhaps millions died to build this defense network. Today, the preferred building materials are missiles, fighter bombers, and atomic warheads — weapons of massive destruction that will kill millions of people in seconds. However, China isn't just seeking star wars technology. It is building up huge conventional forces to take advantage of its greatest resource — a huge population. A lot of the weapons factories are turning out the small arms and supplies needed to equip the largest infantry of all time.

Re-arming China is particularly strange and un-called-for at this point in history. America's monumental defeat in Vietnam reconfirmed what every would-be conqueror has learned about China's virtual hegemony over the Far East: ground invasions against the Chinese are un-winnable. The dragon boasts the largest standing army on earth. Yet he has more than just massive numerical superiority. He has a secret weapon: the national will to shed as much blood as necessary to turn back any invader.

One retired U.S. Marine colonel explained it to me this way, "If the Chinese high command ordered the Red Army to march six abreast off a cliff, they could march for eternity and never catch up with the male birthrate!"

For U.S. strategic planners, this is one of the most sobering considerations preventing any 21st century military confrontation with the Chinese. "It's either pray or become prey," said another pessimistic insider. "When it comes to a war in Asia, the United States can never win on the ground!"

Most Washington military planners cannot project the next 100 years without some kind of confrontation with China. War with China is inevitable for the USA unless we can create a new military alliance between the United States and China. This is why building greater co-dependence is the logic and urgency behind our government's current "China Policy." That is what is happening today under the cover of "engaging China through trade." In the new Asia Pacific balance of power, many U.S. military and political leaders believe the USA will either become China's ally or its victim.

Placating China became one of President Clinton's first assignments after re-election to his second term in office. The U.S. secretary of state and the president flew to Asia to meet with Chinese leaders, assuring them that the United States does not object to peaceful Chinese "expansionism" and again assured Li Ping that the United States is not trying to "contain" China. President Clinton again went out of his way to assure the Chinese that trade will not be re-linked to the growing human rights violations on the mainland.

For now, the United States is determined to build a strategic alliance with China — no matter how inhumane the government in Beijing becomes. It makes both economic and military sense. So the dragon has the message he wants and needs to hear in order to stoke the furnaces of war: "America is willing to sacrifice its most sacred values to placate the hardliners."

Three Decades of Peace

Sane observers wonder why China would plan for war at the same time it is prospering through the current "Pacific peace dividend." Such ingenue thinking shows only that State Department humanists can't understand the depth of evil that motivates the dragon's war plans. He is history's greatest war lover. His talk of peace is only a prelude to making war. Violence is still the only way of "life" he knows. Like Adolf Hitler and the Nazis, peace negotiations are still only war at the conference table instead of war on the field. The Christian knows this because it is revealed in the Word of God — not in history, not at the United Nations, nor at the peace tables or parliaments of this world system.

Today, the fact is that China has no need to fear aggression from the USA or any other nation state. As a result of the Nixon-Kissinger accords with China, the Western alliance has redefined the mission of the Southeast Asia Treaty Organization (SEATO). It no longer maintains the cold war "ring of fire" around China.

While the USA still controls the skies and sea lanes of the Pacific through atomic weapons and satellite technology, this in no way challenges China's territorial integrity or the ability to reach out and trade. This is evident in China's anti-American propaganda. Far from seeing the USA as an enemy, the Chinese portray the USA as a mentally retarded giant — a decadent, immoral society without spiritual direction or national will. Since Vietnam, the United States has never been portrayed as a military threat. Mao was right. We are a paper tiger, only brought out when Beijing needs to manufacture an enemy.

China's Renewed Russian Alliance

They view the Russians as being in similar decay and disarray. In fact, Russia is again an ally — not an enemy — just as the Bible predicts. In April 1996 Beijing renewed its treaty bonds with Moscow, weakened by Henry Kissinger during the Cold War. This new non-aggression pact with their former Communist rival sets the military train back on the track for Apocalypse.

The Chinese now view the Russians not as foes, but as a cheap source of technology such as SU-27 jet fighters, attack submarines, and intercontinental missiles. The 2,700-mile border they share has never been more peaceful.

Significantly, under this renewed treaty with China, the former Soviet republics of Central Asia also renewed their long-term alliance with the Chinese. Nothing is more significant from a biblical perspective. This treaty paves the way for multi-lateral alliances between Beijing and other northern nations of the former USSR. Such alliance are essential for China's participation in the Battle of Armageddon.

What about India?

India is the only other neighbor mentioned as an "external threat" — probably because only India has the numbers needed to challenge China. Its largely Hindu population will soon equal or excel the Chinese. But the two countries have mutually checkmated each other, both having the A-bomb and huge populations to throw into any war effort.

What's more, the Chinese dragon's de-facto alliance with the Islamic world guarantees that India would be isolated in any war with Beijing. For example, China is actively helping the Pakistanis develop a nuclear arsenal aimed at India with barely a protest from the United States. Afghanistan, Bangladesh, and the other Muslim neighbors of India would likely join the Chinese if it came down to a war with the Hindus — a highly unlikely scenario. (While the spirits behind Hinduism are given to violent fits of rage, they serve the dragon, too!) Most Asians accept the non-aggressive policies of India's Hindus at face value. For this reason alone, no serious military planner really considers India a threat to China.

Internal Security Certain

So, if there are no viable external foes, why are the "Double Dragons" of China still rearming? I don't think the Chinese themselves know the real answer. They are mindlessly following a path to mass destruction already laid out by generations of wrong choices. Perhaps Beijing's leaders instinctively know the dragon will double-cross them at some point. Unless they are very good Bible students, most Chinese will never understand their national destiny.

Secondly, military "modernization" is not needed for any domestic threats either. Although China has suffered terrible civil wars throughout the last 4,000 years — and the collective memories of these are great — the dragon has finally united China into one people.

The endemic civil unrest that has always cursed the Chinese people appears over. Until recently, Chinese history read like one endless civil war. Chaos has been endemic — always seething just below the surface. The dragon is always there, growling and rumbling, in the collective soul of China. And the casualties of these outbreaks have been horrific. For example, when Hong Xiuquan led the Taiping Revolt against the Qing dynasty from 1850 to 1864, it left 20 million dead! And that was only one of many civil wars in the 19th century.

The Communist/Nationalist Revolution went on to kill five times as many people. This is especially true if one counts the Great Leap Forward famines of 1960-61, the Cultural Revolution, and endless purges of political and religious dissenters. And it wasn't just the Communists who killed. The Nationalists had their share of atrocities. But today, nobody wants to go back to that. The Chinese are one nation at last.

In fact, people young and old grudgingly accept terrible events like the Tiananmen Square student massacre as necessary for peace. They would rather have mock trials and jailings of dissidents like Wang Dan than chance another "Cultural Revolution." The people of China no longer want anything resembling a civil war, and are seeking instead a new "guoqing" or "Chinese-ness." Though undefined, it stresses a new anti-foreign, anti-western nationalism and traditional Taoist and Confucian values such as "submission" and "obedience."

Tibetan nationalism, "working class" unrest, and tribal minorities are often cited as other internal security threats. However, extensive PSB police infiltration prevents any serious arming or uniting of these groups.

Other factors have united China as well. An immense network of CPC grassroots spy organizations act as "neighborhood watches" to make sure that no opposition voice is heard. Nationally controlled education and media, an interstate highway system, and the world's best central administration all work against civil disorder. For the first time, the whole country speaks one dialect: Mandarin. National television networks are doing in China what they did in the USA during the 1950s, creating an enlarged national consciousness and language. Today, China is laying down the most extensive telecommunications web on planet Earth, another guarantee of growing unity and central control.

When all else fails to quell dissent, there is always the "laogai" prison system. This network of concentration camps uses "re-education through slave labor" to break the spirits and bodies of anyone who opposes the dragon's plans for destroying China.

Practical and businesslike, capitalist Hong Kong is quietly submitting to the dragon's rule. It has never been a serious military threat — even under British rule. No, the dragon doesn't need this arms buildup for internal security reasons either.

What about Taiwan?

Taiwanese nationalism remains a thorn, particularly in the side of the hardline communists. But again, it is not a military threat. Should China attack, a military defense would be suicidal for Taiwan. The Red Army outmans the Taiwanese by 8-1. China outspends Taiwan 3-1 in military spending. The nationalists have no bombers or missiles to attack the mainland, and their jet fighters are outnumbered 12-1!

Though Beijing would ultimately win any war with Taiwan, there are many reasons why it, too, does not want to invade. Next to Hong Kong, Taiwan is the largest outside investor in China's economy. To attack Taiwan would be literally shooting oneself in the foot economically. It would also upset China's neighbors in the entire region, and inflame anti-Chinese militarism among the "little tigers" of Korea, Malaysia/Singapore, Thailand, and Vietnam. Unless China deliberately wanted to provoke an arms race with its neighbors (which it might want to do!) attacking Taiwan is out of the question.

Perhaps that's why the Chinese are making the future of Taiwan into a major bargaining chip with the United States. Assuring peaceful reunification will be a big goal, and given the mood of the recent American administrations, it's probably something the Chinese can have if they want it.

What about Border Security?

China has unsettled territorial disputes with 10 of her 12 neighbors, and claims 2 million square kilometers outside her present-day borders. However, Beijing knows that no one is planning to provoke the dragon with a border attack.

Nor does China give any indication that it wants to reopen old wounds by attacking neighbors or even supporting guerrilla rebellions as it has in the past. The 1960's "peoples wars of liberation" are no longer part of Chinese foreign policy. Just as an attack on Taiwan would trigger a regional arms race against China, any attack by the dragon on its neighbors now would prompt economic reprisals.

What's more, an attack on a neighbor like Korea, the Philippines, or Vietnam would invite increased United States and UN forces into the Pacific. China has already signaled the North Koreans that they cannot count on Chinese support for an attack on Seoul.

So once again, there can be no justification for

increased Chinese militarism based on border threats. What's more, a good argument against this is often made from Chinese history. The present Chinese government has nearly reached the limits of historical borders.

In the past, Chinese emperors have rarely sought territorial control of India, Indonesia, Japan, the Middle East, or even most of Southeast Asia. This would require a strong Navy, something China has never developed. Today, it would also require incredible air power. Unless a new imperialism is brewing (and there is no evidence of that) it is unlikely that China has the will to re-arm for regional conquest. Why conquer when it already has virtual hegemony without paying the price of keeping the peace?

So, we're back where we started. For the first time in history, China is without any viable enemies, yet still prepares for war on an unprecedented scale. Something big is happening here — bigger than even the Chinese themselves realize. And China isn't just building a huge ground force. In the face of worldwide condemnation, it is the only major power still determined to go ahead with the nuclear arms race.

Why Nuclear Arms?

Why does the Chinese dragon still insist on moving ahead with atomic weapons testing and developing delivery systems? If not for the Indians or Russians, who is the target?

The Chinese have given numerous reasons to try to explain this. They say it is for peaceful uses such as "civil engineering" or to protect the earth from straying meteorites! Any day, we can expect them to say they want to provide protection from attacking aliens — which is closer to the truth than most of the Chinese generals realize. (Antichrist may well portray the King of kings and His heavenly hosts as attacking aliens — a version popularly being portrayed in Hollywood films such as *Independence Day*.)

However, the Chinese tipped their atomic hand in March 1996. That's when President Clinton sent the U.S. Pacific fleet into the Taiwan Straits as China tried to stop the presidential elections in Taiwan. It was then that hardline Chinese leaders warned the USA to stop — or face atomic attack on Los Angeles, California! (Choosing the Port of Los Angeles as a target is ironic. The Alameda Corridor is the main import pipeline for Chinese products coming into the USA. Besides killing millions of Americans, such an attack would cripple Chinese trade with the USA for decades.)

That was the first time the media learned that China had plans for targeting the USA with atomic bombs. Who else? It's the only "first strike" objective that would require stars war technology and ICBM delivery systems. In a biblical, end-times scenario, delivering such a knock-out atomic punch to Israel's chief ally would help kill three birds with one stone.

First, it would speed the destruction of Israel. China is an implacable foe of the Jewish state. She is firmly allied with the Russians and Muslim world against the state of Israel. In any war against Israel, it will be important to first knock out American missile capability against Russia and her allies like China, Iraq, and Iran.

Second, to support its own invasion of the Middle East, it will need a strong deterrent against U.S. intervention. Any massive movement of Chinese troops and material to the Middle East would be an easy target for U.S. strategic forces — so they must be destroyed or checkmated with atomic blackmail.

Third, the U.S. naval and nuclear presence in the Pacific is the only barrier preventing real Chinese hegemony over all Asia. China must move toward nuclear and technical parity with the USA if it someday wants the USA out of the Pacific forever.

Nuclear Judgment on the United States

A nuclear first strike on the United States would fit into the pattern of national judgments established since Old Testament times. A "churched" or "Christianized" nation with the mandate to reach another nation for Christ is often the first victim of the unconverted people it fails to reach with the truth.

I believe we are the Church and the nation that God intends to use to reach China. History has placed us in position to pass the baton of the gospel to Asia. The Church in America is logically the most responsible for reaching the Pacific rim (and perhaps the Muslim world) with the gospel. If we fail in our historical destiny, we are inviting judgment.

In their book *Be a Part of It!* Robby and Jackie Butler challenge us to see ourselves this way in Christian history; to view national churches, like the believers here in America, as part of God's gradual redemption of this planet and the human race.[1]

Genesis 1-11 reveals God's plan to extend His reign throughout the earth. Instead, through Adam's rebellion, we were alienated from Him. In order to reach the ones he loved so much on Calvary, God spread the human race around the world and divided them into more-manageable nations. These are the 12,000 "people groups" or "language groups" we know today. Ever since creating this "ethno-linguistic" diversity, God has been redeeming them one by one. His plan is to separate out a people who respond to His grace in each of the tribes and nations. We call these people "the Church" or "called out" ones in each nation.

God choose Abraham, the father of faith, to begin this missionary task through the patriarchs from 2000 to 1600 B.C. (Xia dynasty in China). Christians, including believers in China and the USA, are his modern day descendants. We are still charged to help carry this commission of love to unreached people groups; to love and bless the unreached nations. There are 75 unreached people groups in China alone. Today, Chinese native missionaries can go to them with our "partnership" help.[2]

The dragon knows this, and that's why he wants to cut off all partnership and contact between Christians in China and Christians in the rest of the world. If we allow the dragon to win by stopping missions, then God will find another way for us to reach China.

When Abraham and his children failed to live holy lives and reach their world with the light, God permitted them to be taken captive by the Egyptians. They became slaves of the very people to whom they should have been missionaries! Through this they developed into spiritual leaders of a sort, and the Egyptians finally acknowledged the one true God after Moses' witness. (1600 to 1200 B.C., Shang dynasty).

During the Exodus many unreached nations learned to fear the Lord. God gave the Jews a strategic, central location in Palestine from which to proclaim His name. We have been given such a place in history now, and we need to learn from what happened to the Jews. Instead of glorifying Him, they repeatedly brought dishonor to His name. This went on throughout the period of the Judges (1200-800 B.C., Shang and Western Zhou dynasties), the Kings (800-400 B.C., Eastern Zhou dynasty) and the Post-exile (400-0 B.C., Qin and Western Han dynasties).

So the Philistines, Assyria, Babylon, and Rome were allowed to attack Israel and Judah. It was the only way that God could disperse them to be His witnesses. They failed to voluntarily evangelize their neighbors, to be salt and light, so God allowed them to be defeated and taken captive. This happened again and again until all the world knew about the one true God of the Jews.

Other examples are spread across the pages of history. When the Romans failed to pass along the gospel to Europe, God stirred up the Goths to come and take the Gospel from them (A.D. 0-400, Eastern Han, Three Kingdoms, Western Jin and Eastern Jin dynasties). When the Celts, Goths, and others failed to evangelize Europe, they in turn were attacked by heathen tribes from A.D. 400-800 (Southern and Northern, Sui, and Tang dynasties).

Later, when the Anglos and Celts failed to reach the Vikings, the Norse unwittingly came after the gospel through 250 years of bloody attacks on Britain and France, (A.D. 800-1200, Tang, Five Dynasties, Northern Song, and Golden Tartars dynasties). Eventually, they, too, came to love and glorify God.

Then Europe failed to reach the Sarens with the gospel through the misguided Crusades (A.D. 1200-

1600, during the Southern Song, Yuan, Ming, and Qing dynasties). The result of those ungodly attempts to win Muslims with the sword, and the continued failure to reach Muslims through the following generations, can be seen on CNN television every day! Islamic fundamentalists are in an undeclared war on the West. The attack on God's people by the Jihad continues as you read.

It is no accident that Chinese-style Marxism and Islamic fundamentalists are allies against the United States and Europe — nation states which they consider to be Christian. When the Church fails to be a missionary force, it brings military judgment upon the entire culture and society in which it resides.

Judgment Begins with the House of God

Thus America's backslidden churches are bringing wrath on the United States, since the Bible says that judgment always begins with the house of God (1 Peter 4:17). There is a very strong possibility that at some point soon, God will allow China to deliver economic or military justice to the people of the United States. The American church, which God has blessed to be the light of the world, will receive judgment if it refuses to support missions and charity abroad — especially in the countries of the Pacific rim.

After so many years of abortion murders, treaty-breaking, and warmongering — the USA's "sex and death" culture has stored up a frightening blood guilt. This iniquity is so great that soon only recession, military defeat or natural disaster will be able to erase the national debt. To right the scales of justice, a ground invasion of the United States might be permitted, and

China is the only super-power with the force available to punish the USA.

America, which has invaded so many other countries, could be invaded herself. It is not hard to imagine the Chinese being able to launch such an attack on the West Coast. Atomic explosions in the atmosphere over the United States would knock out our high-tech communications systems. Without a star-wars defense to stop the Chinese and their Russian allies, the Chinese infantry would have instant ground superiority. The technical superiority we trust in now would thus prove to be our greatest weakness! This is the Taoist way of warfare, to use the opponents strength against him.

Other delivery systems are possible as well. Chinese terrorists could assemble atomic weapons or release germ warfare within the United States. China's Russian allies might also re-target the United States for atomic attack before attacking Israel, thus opening the door for a Chinese invasion force.

Perhaps it won't get that far. Even the threat of ground invasion might be enough to bring the USA to its knees. Antichrist, pretending to be a peace-maker, may be able to form a temporary international alliance or treaty between the United States and China. Perhaps current negotiations between China and the USA will make us firm allies before the end-time Battle of Armageddon. Both nations may surrender their atomic weapons to some kind of United Nations control which Antichrist can use to establish his world capital in Israel. For a time, the United States and China might even join in an international peacekeeping force.

Of course, it's most likely that the USA will surrender sovereignty to the Antichrist's one world government and join his European alliance — postponing potential conflict with China until Armageddon. There is going to be mind-numbing international diplomacy before that final battle begins. Antichrist will form, break, and reform alliances in order to concentrate massive firepower in the Middle East. During the entire "countdown to Armageddon" period, the USA will remain vulnerable to atomic attack.

How Does Armageddon Fit?

However it happens, we can be certain of an enormous Chinese presence at the final Battle of Armageddon. The Kings of the East are destined to supply 200 million soldiers — and no one but China is capable of mobilizing such forces. Thus, China will unwittingly fall into Antichrist's agenda for a united worldwide defense against "an alien attack" from outer space. It's very possible that Chinese soldiers and their allies will be so deceived that they won't even know their real enemy or that they are actually being tricked into coming to battle Christ and His heavenly hosts.

The Bible doesn't explain exactly how the dragon will finally lure 200 million oriental cavalry and infantry to Armageddon — but he will. The dragon understands the Chinese mind. End-times author and expert John Hagee believes the best explanation is oil. China will lead an all-Asia alliance simply to protect the free flow of Middle Eastern crude. Of course, the Chinese, their East and Southeast Asian hegemony, and the Japanese all depend on outside oil for daily survival. The argument has some merit. Oil could be the spark that ignites this war.

China's international treaties almost guarantee such

involvement. Beijing has strong alliances with the non-aligned and Muslim nations (Kings of the South) and with the Russians (Kings of the North). Like the Russians and Africans, China will be strongly motivated to keep Antichrist's ten-nation European alliance from gaining control over that oil. If the West did control the oil cartel, China's industry would be reduced to near-slavery. This would be especially true mid-way through the Tribulation when so much of its infrastructure has been destroyed through natural calamities.

Others suggest that powerful Muslim influences in South Asia and Indonesia will draw the Kings of the East to Armageddon. They will be enraged by Antichrist's blasphemy at the Dome of the Rock, and eager to dislodge him from Muslim shrines in the Holy Land. Perhaps some Chinese Muslim Ugyurs might join for this reason — or China's alliances with Islamic states might come into play.

Yet it would have to be more than just oil, or what's left of the Islamic Jihad and China's other Pan-African alliances. Remember Armageddon is China's largest-ever military adventure outside her borders — and the first expeditionary force to travel so far.

It is not hard for me as a Chinese to imagine the only kind of propaganda that will inflame China into launching such a transcontinental crusade. By the time China mobilizes the People's Liberation Army to attack the Antichrist's capital at Jerusalem, Chinese nationalism will be at a feverish pitch. And this nationalism will not be trumped-up emotionalism. No, by then the Chinese will have discovered that Antichrist's one-world government condemns them to humiliating poverty and servitude.

China is capable of mobilizing the patriotic frenzy needed for Armageddon. My people have done it in the past when threatened with extinction. And that's exactly how this will appear. By being forced into the Antichrist's scheme for one-world government, one-world religion, and one-world economy, the people of China will see themselves once again in total bondage to an essentially Western alliance. The dragon's mask will be ripped off at last — and he will have round eyes! China will understand that all along, the Antichrist dragon has been an outside force. In the Chinese slang of hatred, Antichrist will be a green-eyed, foreign devil. China will lose great face, realizing that they have been emotionally exploited and manipulated by the Antichrist, and their rage will be uncontrollable.

China's free trade with the rest of the world will end with the fall of economic Babylon (Rev. 14:8). China's culture, religions, and philosophies will be absorbed into Antichrist's one-world religion overnight. China's hard-won sovereignty will be lost. In short, Antichrist will destroy both the pride of new China and glory of old China. The Chinese will not stand for this. They will be unwilling to again lose control of their destiny — especially after having paid such a terrible price to free themselves from the humiliation of 19th century colonialism.

No wonder China will turn on this man the Bible has code-named the Antichrist. In fact, this may be why the Bible says that the movement of Oriental kings against Antichrist will "trouble him" (Rev. 16:12; Dan. 11:44). Perhaps he didn't expect resurgent nationalism in the Orient to be so strong.

However, it won't trouble the Antichrist for long.

He will cunningly use it. The Chinese may think they are coming to Israel to attack him, but the Antichrist will end up turning them toward "the dark side" — to attack the returning Christ. That's the tragedy of China. The Middle Kingdom's terrible prophetic destiny is to sacrifice the largest army in history resisting the King of kings and Lord of lords! It will be China's last attempt to stop the kingdom of Cathay from becoming the kingdom of God.

Before the dragon is finally thrown into the Lake of Fire for 1,000 years, he intends to drag this last human landslide of souls down with him. Antichrist hates the Chinese people to the very end. This will be his final evil trick on the Han nation — and all the people groups of China.

This is why supporting native Chinese missionaries is so important to me, and why my mother and I started the Love China Club back in 1994. That's why it is so important to us that we print and distribute hundreds of millions of Bibles in China now.

Time is running out for China. The sands of time are sinking for all the peoples of Asia. Hundreds of millions of Chinese souls are about to plunge into eternity without ever knowing the Christ who alone can save them. This is why oriental missions have to be "priority one" for the end-times church. Chinese support must be our last great missionary thrust from the USA.

In spite of the fact that American missionaries are currently banned from China, India, and so many Asian countries — we are still welcome in Asia. Americans and American dollars are much-valued right now as tourists and investment partners in the future of the

"Pacific rim." No one has greater access to Asia's unreached millions than the American people. We must enter this open door before it is too late. Short-term mission teams, itinerant ministries, and co-venture partnerships with indigenous churches and mission agencies are welcome. Christ warned us to work for Him during periods of freedom and "daylight" hours because he knew that a spiritual "nightfall" is coming to Asia when "no man can work" (John 9:4).

Steps to Armageddon

Armageddon is not one battle, says John Hagee in *Beginning of the End,* but 42 months of warfare. It begins halfway through the Great Tribulation, after Russia and the Islamic Jihad have been nearly destroyed in their own disastrous war of genocide against the state of Israel.[3]

By then Satan and his host of dark angels will have been defeated in the heavens and cast down to earth. Satan, with the help of Antichrist and the false prophet, will intensify his attacks on Christian converts in China and worldwide (Rev. 13:7).

Wars, plagues, and catastrophes will kill at least 700 million Chinese during this period. The death toll in the coastal cities across Asia will be staggering as ports flood. In cities like Bangkok, Hanoi, Ho Chi Ming, Hong Kong, Guangzhou, Manila, Shanghai, and Yangoon the death toll will climb to over 50 million! Not just China's ports — but nearly every Asian nation and seaport will have suffered similar death tolls. In cities like Calcutta and Dacca the new shorelines may extend 70 to 100 miles inland. The dead and refugees will be incalculable.

Atomic fallout, germ warfare, and environmental poisoning will have spread throughout the Asia Pacific rim. "Red Tide" pollution will wipe out fishing in many areas of Asia which depend on seafood. Mass starvation will be inevitable.

In archipelagos like Indonesia, Japan, the Philippines, Taiwan, and Singapore, the death toll will reach as high as 364 million. Many South Sea islands will disappear forever (Rev. 16:20) in a series of massive geological and astronomical changes.

A series of unprecedented earthquakes will level the world's tallest buildings in Beijing, Hong Kong, Malaysia, and Shanghai (Rev. 16:17-21). The high-rise temples of trade that have become the symbols of modernization will be shaken to pieces. Ancient landmarks like the Great Wall, Temple of Heaven, and Ming Tombs will be destroyed forever. The new airports, bridges, dams, and high-tech infrastructure recently built by China's civil engineers will become piles of rubble. The Lord Jesus predicted destruction so severe in Matthew 24 that not one stone would remain upon another stone. I believe that prediction about the Jerusalem temple also applies to many other temples ancient and modern throughout Asia.

The Battle of Armageddon

While all this global destruction continues, China leads the Kings of the East to form a new military alliance. They will join Beijing, first in worldwide war against the Antichrist and then in war on the Lord Jesus himself. Let me explain how this amazing switch occurs.

In the first "world war" against Israel, predicted in

Ezekiel 38 and 39, the Chinese avoid direct ground involvement. As much as China hates Israel, the Antichrist has not yet touched the hot button that sets off the fury of China.

Although Antichrist doesn't lift a finger to fulfill his peace treaty obligations to defend Israel from the Russian/Muslim Jihad, God supernaturally intervenes to defend the Jews. The Russian and Muslim allies suffer 84 percent casualties in the battle. The carnage is so terrible that clean-up teams take seven months just to bury the dead — and another seven years to burn their weapons!

Antichrist understands how precarious is his position. Flushed with excitement over the newly-weakened Muslim and Russian positions, he decides now is the moment to consolidate global power in an unprecedented bold step.

Antichrist's Attack on China

Underestimating the nationalism of the Chinese Axis, Antichrist uses the wonder of his resurrection from the dead (Rev. 13:3) to stage a coup against the world-system the Bible codenames Babylon. This is the global alliance of business, government and religion that put him into power in the first place! And it is a world system that superpower China will participate in fully and helped to develop. The Antichrist's assault on "Babylon" is twofold:

(1) RELIGIOUS ATTACK — Antichrist substitutes the worship of Satan for the gods of the world church (religious Babylon). This is done by setting up his image in the temple at Jerusalem, a blasphemy not only against Jehovah God, but also against Allah and the

Lord Jesus Christ. In China, this is an affront to both Christians and traditional Chinese religions. The Chinese churches are nevertheless forced to merge into one world church. The Three Self-Patriotic Buddhists, Three Self-Patriotic Catholics, and Three Self-Patriotic Protestants are all made one under Antichrist's new world church. Chinese who convert to Christ in these days rather than worship the dragon's image will face execution in the final, most terrible religious persecution of Chinese history.

(2) COMMERCIAL ATTACK — Then, the Antichrist takes over commercial Babylon by establishing a world bank using the mark of the beast. China's powerful, independent, market-driven economy is no more. By controlling both currency and religious culture, Antichrist tries to rule the world right down to the Chinese village level.

For the first half of the seven-year tribulation, economic and religious Babylon ruled the world, including Antichrist. Now the Babylonian system that enriched China for thousands of years and guided her way of life has been destroyed. Remember, it is the Babylon market culture — not Marxism or capitalism — which has always ruled Chinese civilization and economy.

To restore this rule, China and all the Asian tigers she dominates decide to act militarily. They align themselves with the remnants of the Russian and African forces to drive Antichrist out of Israel forever. Their ultimate goal? To re-establish and revive the global Babylonish systems they have known and loved for years.

Since the Chinese military was not directly involved on the ground during the first attack on Israel, that defeat of the Russian and Muslim coalitions leaves the Oriental axis the strongest military force on earth!

Only Antichrist controls a military and police force nearly equal to China's superpower force. So the united "Army of the Orient" remains the lone challenger to the military power of Antichrist — the last superpower. The remnants of the Russian and Islamic armies have no one to look to for leadership now except China. There is no other source of future reinforcements. They join the Chinese forces, obviously for another attempt to destroy Israel and internationalize Jerusalem. And of course, they, too, need to throw off the yoke of Antichrist.

The Greatest Attack in History

The Pan-Islamic and African forces move up toward Israel, probably joining China and the Asian alliance at Kuwait to march up the Euphrates River valley. Supernaturally dried up from earthquakes and dams, the riverbed permits the combined forces to move rapidly up toward Jerusalem. It becomes a highway of doom for the Red Army. (As I was typing this chapter, we heard a radio report that the middle-eastern nations were angry at Turkey for building dams that are drying up the Euphrates! Biblical prophecy is being fulfilled at a dizzying rate. Piece by piece, each Scripture is coming to pass.)

Meanwhile, Russia's surviving expeditionary forces join with the Kings of the North to come down and join the Chinese on the plains of Meggido. There, hundreds of millions of men and weapons converge, seeking to meet the high-tech "peace keeping" forces of Antichrist's

European alliance. The Bible says these armies cover the earth from the plains north of Palestine, through the valley of Jehoshaphat near Jerusalem and all the way down to the land of Edom.

There, instead of clashing with each other, they come face to face with a new enemy — Christ at his second coming. The description in Revelation 19:11-21 predicts the grisly results:

> And I saw heaven opened, and behold a white horse; and he that sat upon him was called Faithful and True, and in righteousness he doth judge and make war.
>
> His eyes were as a flame of fire, and on his head were many crowns; and he had a name written, that no man knew, but he himself.
>
> And he was clothed with a vesture dipped in blood: and his name is called The Word of God.
>
> And the armies which were in heaven followed him upon white horses, clothed in fine linen, white and clean.
>
> And out of his mouth goeth a sharp sword, that with it he should smite the nations: and he shall rule them with a rod of iron: and he treadeth the winepress of the fierceness and wrath of the Almighty God.
>
> And he hath on his vesture and on his thigh a name written, KING OF KINGS, AND LORD OF LORDS.
>
> And I saw an angel standing in the sun; and he cried with a loud voice, saying to all the fowls that fly in the midst of heaven, Come

and gather yourselves together unto the supper of the great God;

That he may eat the flesh of kings and the flesh of captains, and the flesh of mighty men, and the flesh of horses and of them that sit on them, and the flesh of all men, both free and bond, both small and great.

And I saw the beast, and the kings of the earth, and their armies, gathered together to make war against him that sat on the horse, and against his army.

And the beast was taken, and with him the false prophet that wrought miracles before him, with which he deceived them that had received the mark of the beast, and them that worshipped his image. these both were cast alive into a lake of fire burning with brimstone.

And the remnant were slain with the sword of him that sat upon the horse, which sword proceeded out of his mouth: and all the fowls were filled with their flesh.

Revelation 14:20 predicts a river of blood flowing from this confrontation. It is so deep it rises up to horses bridles for nearly 200 miles!

To any of my fellow Chinese who are reading these words, let me say one thing: it is not too late for you! If you can still read this, there is still time. You don't have to join in this slaughter.

It is not too late for you to accept the love and mercy of Christ before He comes in judgment to rule the world. If you accept Him early enough, you can join Him at the marriage feast of the Lamb. Millions of Christians will be raptured from the earth and avoid the terrors of the Tribulation and Armageddon. Many of these will be Chinese.

Perhaps by the time you read this book, Antichrist already rules the earth. The events described in this book will happen soon — in this generation! It is possible that many reading these pages will go through some of the hellish experiences described in the Bible, in Revelation 6 to 19. Your Christian friends and the true church of Christ may be gone by the time you read this page. Even then it is not too late for you to accept Christ's love and mercy. The body they may kill, but God's truth abideth still.

Dear reader, won't you accept Jesus Christ as your King of kings and Lord of lords right now? Simply pray the following prayer. Mean it with all your heart.

The Sinner's Prayer

Almighty God and creator of the world, I confess that I have sinned against You and my neighbors. I have not kept Your laws. I believe that You sent the Lord Jesus Christ to die on Calvary to satisfy my debt and die in my place. I receive You, Lord Jesus Christ, as my Lord God and Saviour. Wash me in Your blood and adopt me into Your family as You promised. Give me the grace to live for You and welcome me into heaven to live forever when I depart this life. In Jesus' name, Amen.

[1]Robby and Jackie Butler, *Be a Part of It!* (Pasadena, CA: U.S. Center for World Mission, 1996), p. 9-10.

[2]Joshua Project 2000 Unreached Peoples List, p.2, A.D. 2000 & Beyond Movement, Colorado Springs, CO, 1996.

[3]John Hagee, *Beginning of the End* (Nashville, TN: Thomas Nelson Publishers, 1996).

Chapter 4

The Dragon's Worst Nightmare: the Soon Return of Jesus Christ

For just as the lightning comes from the east, and flashes to the west, so shall the coming of the Son of Man be (Matt. 24:29;NASB).

At least once a year over the past decade, I have been privileged to sit under the end-times teaching of Reverend Lin Xiangao, the most famous of all the Chinese house pastors. Known in the West as Samuel Lamb or simply "Pastor Lamb," he suffered over 20 years in the dread "Bamboo Gulag" labor camps. His dear wife did not survive and died for her faith in Christ. Today, Pastor Lamb is known as the underground Bishop of Canton and the Billy Graham of China.

Whenever I bring American Christians to visit the Pearl River port of Guangzhou, we always climb the narrow, steep stairs that lead to his crowded church loft. If China had such memorials, this would deserve to be a national shrine. As Anne Frank's house is a memorial to the victims of the Jewish holocaust, his humble flat should be a monument to the suffering of China's underground church. It is sacred space — and still home to the large underground congregation he shepherds.

Lamb's loft has become one of the most publicized and popular tourist attractions in southern China! Almost daily, he welcomes a steady stream of pilgrims from around the world. They come to see a "real house church" but instead they get a Bible class. The subject is always the same: every Christian's "end-times hope."

Rapt visitors sit slackjawed in worshipful awe as he shares the secrets of Chinese pietism. He is always kind and tender toward those who have caused him so much pain. I have never once heard him criticize the people who sentenced him and his wife to the prison where she died a martyr.

Yet he is faithful to preach a gospel that is almost forgotten in the United States and Europe. He never fails to reveal how and why China's underground church is exploding — and why Chinese Christians have grown so strong under persecution. Most American Christians miss the point of his patient talks. No matter how carefully they listen to his saintly teaching, most still don't get the point!

The Secret Hope of the Chinese Church

The teachings of Pastor Lamb and Chinese martyrs like Watchman Nee and Wang Mingdao seem strangely "other-worldly" to most American visitors. But not for the frustrated Communist cadre assigned to stop the gospel they teach. They know there is a living God because they can't stop His powerful Word.

The hardliners in Beijing have learned that "the most dangerous message in the most dangerous book" is being taught by these house church pastors! No wonder they're still raiding thousands of house churches even as I write — 17,900 were shut down in Zhejiang Province alone during one recent anti-Christian campaign, according to official government reports.[1] All this effort, just to stop unregulated Bible studies.

In the West, we think of bomb-making instructions on the Internet as dangerous. Not to the dragon. To him, the "most dangerous" message on the Internet is the "Second Advent of Christ." The soon return of Christ is the message the PSB thought-police most want to censor out. In fact, in many areas the police are registering modems and even fax machines in order to keep the end-times message of Christ's return from being circulated.

You see, Chinese Christians believe passionately that Christ is coming again, not just someday — but "in this generation." The dragon knows he must stop this Apostolic message of hope. If somehow he can stop these New Testament-style Bible studies, he knows he will cripple Church growth in China.

That's why peaceful, gentle old men like Pastor Lamb are still marked for persecution in today's China.

Between interviews for this book last year, police raiders again confiscated Bibles and books from his apartment. (Reporters in Hong Kong believe he may still be assassinated by secret police, who often make such killings look like suicides or accidents.)

Our problem in the West is different. It is not that we aren't getting the truth. We have it. Our problem is not that we don't have Bibles. We just don't believe them! We especially disbelieve the hundreds of predictions about the coming "Day of the Lord." We ignore Christ's warnings in Matthew 24, Luke 21:34, 2 Peter 3:10, and Revelation 6:17. The Bible clearly warns that Christ's coming will take careless Christians by surprise — coming like a thief in the night.

* Like the five foolish virgins, we Americans aren't waiting for the bridegroom to return at any moment (Matt. 25:11-13).

* Like the preoccupied banquet invitees who scorned the King, we're putting business, career and personal affairs ahead of Christ (Matt. 22:1-6).

* Like the careless dinner guest who didn't dress for dinner, we're not putting on the robes of righteousness we need to meet the Lord at his appearing (Matt. 22: 11-12).

No wonder American visitors ask the wrong questions when we tour the fast-growing house churches of China! We want to hear "practical answers" and success formulas like the spiritual baby food we're used to getting a home in the States. We want to see "how to" human blueprints for why the underground cell churches multiply so quickly. But Pastor Lamb understands the real power of the gospel message — that Christ died, rose from the dead, and is coming again (Heb. 9:28).

That's the simple gospel the Chinese Church believes. And that's why they are growing in numbers and power while the mainline churches in the West are shrinking and weak!

Evangelism In Deed and Word

Pastor Lamb has earned the right to be described as the Chinese Billy Graham. Even though the dragon will not allow him to hold public evangelistic crusades, he is easily the most famous evangelist in China today. His handwritten "end-times gospel" teachings are passed from one underground church to the next.

He has become the modern-day apostle Paul of China, speaking for the Lord much as Paul did during his days of "house arrest" during the Roman persecutions. Even the police and government spies assigned to Pastor Lamb respectfully call him "Uncle." Many are converting to Christ just as the Imperial Guard did in Rome! The more the dragon persecutes house church leaders like him, the faster the unregistered church grows.

The same power that spread the gospel throughout the world in the Book of Acts is available to the Church today. All we have to do is look to China to see that the primitive message has never lost its impact. Christians here in America have a lot to learn from the Church in China.

The "end-times gospel" message has always had far more power than the man who preaches it. "When I am weak," said Paul, "then I am strong." He bragged about preaching the gospel simply without rhetoric or wisdom. Pastor Lamb is living proof of the same principle. Preaching the gospel of 1 Corinthians 15:22-25 has made Pastor

Lamb the nearest thing China has to a national spiritual leader — a kind of Chinese pope! Aging and frail, he wouldn't have the strength to administrate the thousands of congregations he has fathered — even if the Religious Affairs Bureau in Beijing lifted their ban on him. Yet his amazing spiritual influence is greater than ever! All because he teaches that we're terminal — the terminal generation before Christ's return.

If you believe and live out a message like that, there is little the power-brokers of this world can take from you. The dragon's threats fall uselessly to the ground when you believe that to live is Christ and to die is gain (Phil. 1:21).

Preaching a Forbidden Message

That's why Pastor Lamb fearlessly and patiently continues preaching the most forbidden message in China today. And Antichrist is furious about it. Even though the dragon is reluctantly allowing a few Bibles to be printed and legally distributed, he still forbids preaching its message. The kingdom of God and the second coming of Christ are the rarest sermon topics preached in China's government-controlled pulpits. Congregations registered with the Three Self Patriotic Movement will not find these subjects in the lectionary of approved readings. The last book in the Bible — John's Revelation — is the "chapter" that Satan hates to hear the most.

The dragon persecutes the house churches because he is terrified of the end-times gospel they preach. This message liberates the people from bondage to their control and so it has to be denounced as "anti-revolutionary" superstition.

• Christians are consistently forbidden the right to do any public evangelism of any kind. Private worship is reluctantly permitted but gospel preaching is banned.

• Directives to the state-controlled churches warn pastors not to preach the message of Revelation.

• Pastors in congregations of the "Three Self Patriotic movement" skip liturgical readings about the second coming of Christ such as Hebrews 9:28 and Revelation 19 and 22:20-21.

• Sunday school teachers are not allowed to discuss the "Day of the Lord" predicted in both the Old and New Testaments.

• The Olivet Discourse, recorded in three of the four Gospels, is a forbidden text (Matt. 24-25, Mark 13:1-27, and Luke 21:5-36).

• Many Chinese hymns of advent, missions, judgment, and the millennial reign of Christ are no longer sung in registered Chinese churches. Such music isn't politically correct.

Even when a Chinese pastor preaches on the Christian's armor in Ephesians 6, he has to make sure that there are no police spies in the audience. If there are, he must carefully avoid the section on the helmet of salvation. Why? Because the Christian's helmet — the "hope of our salvation" — is nothing less than the soon coming of Christ. Meditate on the power of the Christian's hope in 1 Peter starting from the key verses in chapter 1:3-4. (Many Chinese have memorized the whole book since the dragon took power!)

Nothing so upsets the dragon as the mention of Christ's return, and nothing so comforts the Chinese church and missions. To us it is a day of light and rejoicing, to him a day of darkness and judgment. The dragon hates the announcement of His return, not only because it consigns Antichrist to the Lake of Fire, but because it empowers the Chinese to become overcomers. This happens in two very dramatic ways:

The Gospel Message of End-Times Power

FIRST, IT EMPOWERS THE BELIEVERS BY GIVING THEM COMFORT IN THEIR CURRENT SUFFERINGS. The hope of salvation enables them to bear the pain of persecution. What's more, they are able to get beyond the hurt, and love those who torment them. How do you handle it when your own son or daughter turns you in to the police for being a Christian? The secret is Christ's promise in Matthew 24:34. This time of sorrow is very short. House church pastors like Brother Samuel Lamb are certain that Christ will return in "this generation." They believe we are the generation our Lord was referring to Matthew 24, Mark 13, and Luke 21.

Unlike believers in the USA, the Chinese don't expect the Great Tribulation to come "some day" faraway in the future. In fact, when you cross the border from Hong Kong to China, you immediately understand why many Chinese believe they are already in the Tribulation! Or if not in it now, that it will start very soon. You can actually feel the power of the dragon ruling China — I have heard this testimony repeated hundreds of times by visitors to China. Others have reported seeing visions of a dark cloud over China. The oppression is real. Spiritual people feel it — but Christians also know that it won't last forever! They know God is on the throne, and there is a purpose for their trials and afflictions.

The centralized power, growing militarism, persecutions, and public executions are evidence to them that Antichrist is alive and well on planet Earth. They see him acting to take over the international economy, religion, trade, and government — starting with China. In America, we only study about the terrors of the tribulation. The Church in China is already experiencing them!

Yet China's gentle Christians love their enemies. They know that "we war not against flesh and blood but powers and principalities in heavenly places." They realize that their Communist neighbors are victims of a powerful delusion. This helps them to forgive and overcome those who abuse and hate them.

SECOND, IT GIVES THEM POWERFUL MOTIVATION TO BE MISSIONARIES FOR CHRIST. When you understand that Christ could return today, you become a lover of lost souls. That's why Chinese believers are consumed with reaching their families, friends, and neighbors for Christ. Time is short. Every Chinese believer understands that he or she is a missionary. They are serious about Christ's pleas to "work for the night is coming when no man can work" (John 9:4).

As bad as things are now for evangelism, China's overcoming witnesses know that it is only going to get worse. That's why, whenever government persecution lets up temporarily, they evangelize. Every time they see a little patch of blue sky — any opening for Christ — they are quick to witness for the Lord. So the Church in China just grows and grows and grows. The dragon has taken away all earthly hope from the Chinese. When the end-times Scriptures are made plain, that hope returns. That "blessed hope" is why so many Chinese are turning to Christ — and why the addicted, the poor, the sick, the prisoner, and the outcasts are always drawn to God's love at Calvary.

Defining China's Powerful End-Times Faith

Many Chinese leaders link the birth of New China in 1949 with the restoration of Israel in 1948. The final countdown to Christ's return began, they believe, when the "fig tree" of Matthew 24:32 sprang to life again. That's when Israel was reborn as a nation state. This is the sign the Bible says should encourage us that Christ's return "is very near, at the very doors" (Matt. 24:33).

Meticulous calculations, dating of prophecies, and the study of Jewish prophecies fascinate many Chinese leaders. They are closely watching the prophetic clock through God's dealings with the nation of Israel. Many are so sure of Christ's soon return that they have set dates, a practice which Pastor Lamb warns against.

"We should not predict which day, month, or year Jesus will come back," he writes in letters to the Chinese churches. "Matthew 24:36 tells us that no man knows the day or hour of His return. However, the signs that we see lead us to believe that the return of the Lord is very near."

How near? Pastor Lamb and tens of thousands of other Chinese pastors believe it will be within this generation. He believes Matthew 24:32 does not refer to the age of grace between Christ's resurrection and second coming. It is not a "period" or "dispensation" but a literal generation — our generation.

In the Bible, generation is used to refer to three periods of time, 40 years, 50 years, and 70 years. Since 40 years have passed, Jesus could not have been referring to that use of "generation."

"We hope Jesus is referring to the 50-year generation. This is a year of Jubilee," says Lamb with an ingenious smile, "before 1998!"

If not, he adds quickly, "Jesus was referring to the 70-year generation. Remember, 51 to 69 years is also within the 70 years!" Thus, Christ could return anytime between 1998 and 2020.

China's New Mission-minded Churches

This exciting hope has created wave after wave of missionary zeal in the Chinese Church. Even in Hong Kong, China's new international center of Babylonian materialism, global missions is becoming a much more important part of indigenous church life and thinking. Numerous indigenous Chinese mission agencies are springing up for outreach in the 21st century.

On July 14, 1996, only one year before the return of Hong Kong to Chinese control, over 15,000 Chinese believers gathered in Hong Kong Stadium for a World Missions Rally.

At the close of that historic meeting, over 500 went forward to dedicate themselves to reaching the 1.6 billion people of East Asia with the gospel. Many of these young Chinese know that their decision will mean imprisonment, perhaps death and certainly poverty and hardship. It is a radical world view change for the Church in Hong Kong — away from getting rich to enriching others!

Missiologists welcome this new wave of indigenous missions. There has never been an ethnic or national church like the global Chinese community. Except for the Jews, no nation has preserved a cultural identity for so long. No people group is so numerous, exists in so many regions and countries, speaks so many tongues and dialects, or is blessed with so much talent and wealth.

Through the Chinese, God has already implanted a "fifth column" missionary force throughout the entire "10/40 window" — that area of the globe which mission experts say contains the last unreached tribes and nations. Since Christ said he would not return until the Gospel of the Kingdom has been preached to all nations, the Chinese church is beginning to see that it has a unique spiritual destiny to fulfill (Matt. 24).

Every "Chinatown" from Osaka to Male, from Istanbul to Mogadishu to Dakar is now potentially a mission base for Christ. Chinese Christians from Moscow to New York are learning to reach out to their neighbors — especially those "ethnic Chinese" who are born and raised in the host culture. They hold the keys to reaching their neighbors for Christ.

The Chinese have already gone everywhere and gained acceptance in every culture. Even where American missionaries are no longer welcome, this "Chinese Diaspora" is finding ways to assimilate and flourish as Christian witnesses.

The Chinese Coordinating Centre of World Evangelism (CCCOWE) has published a Chinese language prayer book to help intercessors pray through the gateway cities of the 10/40 window. Just as the Church in the West entered the 20th century with a global vision, it appears that the Church in the Far East is beginning the 21st century led by the same Holy Spirit — possessed by the missionary heart of God.

Could it be that the missionary mantle that rested

on England and the USA in the 19th and 20th centuries has fallen on the shoulders of Asian nations? Is finding ways to support these indigenous missions movements an important strategy for U.S. believers and local churches? I think so. This must be part of our vision and plans for the 21st century.

Chinese Missionaries Going to Central Asia

A group of church leaders in China is already planning to preach the gospel all the way back to Jerusalem according to David Wang of Asian Outreach.[2] He says the movement is one of the common goals of 42 leaders of the charismatic house-church movement representing 21 million believers in 11 Chinese provinces.

Neil Johnson, a short-term missionary, told reporters that the Chinese now want to take the gospel back to where it started and "complete the circle" of Christianity's spread around the world.

Huge networks of military highways, like the interstate system in the United States, are being built along the old Silk Roads leading back to the Mediterranean. China is building roads to Armageddon but they are also roads to world evangelism. New rail and pipelines are also opening vast new trade opportunities between China, Central Asian republics like Turkmenistan, and the Muslim middle-east.

Chinese church planters are planning to set up "stepping stone" congregations along these routes back to Jerusalem. Missionary teams have already been sent to Tajikistan and Uzbekistan. According to Ronald Yu of the U.S. Center for World Mission, the missionaries will probably start by ministering to the large numbers of Chinese expatriates who have emigrated to those countries.

Over 12 countries are in the "10/40 window" border with China. There is no reason to believe that the Chinese will not be able to penetrate these countries with the gospel. Closed societies in the Persian Gulf, Iran, and Iraq have police states quite similar to China's. The Chinese have learned how to cope with religious oppression. China's house church movement is the only way the body of Christ can flourish and grow under such persecution.

Korean and other Asian missionaries to China are already "prayer walking" the Silk Road from Beijing through Xian, Lanzhou, Urumqi, and the Asian republics of Kazakhstan, Uzbekistan, Azerbaijan, and Armenia into Turkey. Going overland, the trip only takes four weeks to get to Israel. All along the way, they are meeting with Chinese house church leaders.

The dream of preaching the gospel along the Silk Route is not new to Chinese evangelists. In the 1930s, a number of Chinese missionaries died attempting to pass through neighboring countries to the far west of China. Some Chinese believers living in Urumqi still recall the teams that went forth at that time.

Increasing Evangelism in China

Meanwhile, underground, itinerant evangelism continues within China at horrific personal sacrifice. China itself remains the largest "unreached" nation if you define it as a "World A" country, just as China remains the largest unreached continent. (According to this popular missions formula, China is still defined as an Unreached People Group because the majority of its members still have little or no access to gospel preaching.)

Taking the commands of Christ literally, thousands of Chinese native evangelists are going from village to village carrying no purse. Traveling in pairs, they reveal the gospel to families who take them in for the night or feed them. Where they are not welcomed, they do not stay. If a village seems too dangerous, they walk on. Sometimes they sleep under the stars or bridges. At other times, they are welcomed into the homes of believers where they teach and meet with cell groups.

In his book, *The Coming Influence of China*, broadcaster Carl Lawrence tells a poignant story of just such an evangelist. A young pastor from Hong Kong was being discipled by the older veteran.

> After two weeks, the young pastor, though greatly refreshed in spirit, had used up all of his physical reserves. "Why do you keep moving so fast?" he asked the evangelist. "Some of the people asked you to stay longer, but each morning before the sun is up you awaken me, and we walk together in the darkness, not sure where we are going — except we know that, since this is China, there will always be another village just down the road. Sometimes that village is very far away. When the sun comes up the days are as hot as the nights are cold."
>
> The pastor attempted to make a slight scratch on the serious veneer with which the evangelist took every question; he tried a

Western expression he had learned: "Relax, man, you're too uptight . . . those villages will still be there tomorrow."

"You are right," the evangelist replied. "The villages will still be there tomorrow, but I am not sure I will still be. You see, my brother, what we are doing is illegal and the police are right behind us. I have not been home for four years. I have a family — two boys, like you. They meet me once in a while in one of the villages where their relatives live, but I know that if I go home I will be arrested."[3]

It is just such dedication that keeps front-line native missionaries in China going. They are willing to pay any price to reach China with the gospel.

Because of their sacrifice, hundreds of thousands of house meetings are being forced to meet underground all over China. It is from these cells that the gospel is being shared through family, business, and friendship networks. That is the Chinese way.

Each mature Christian is prayerfully waiting and looking for opportunities to share Christ with the people in their personal network. These are the proverbial "five people" with whom they "live, work, eat, play, and trade." Everybody has about 20-25 such people in their circle of influence at any point in their lives. By reaching them for Christ, the Chinese are reaching their world! And they are preaching this gospel primarily through the amazing power of the house church movement.

House Churches Model New Life

The Holy Spirit has used the dragon's ferocious persecution of Chinese Christians to revive the first century model for the local Church. It is one that can easily be emulated worldwide, and it is even spreading throughout the United States.

Chinese "House Church groups" have developed an "overcomers" mode of assembling, based on a return to the successful "pre-Constantine" models of evangelism, education, and worship. This primitive, New Testament style church thrives without hierarchy or paid clergy.

As the Communists took power, house church pioneers like Watchman Nee saw that the Chinese would go through a period of persecution much like the early Christians suffered under Nero and the Roman empire — and like the Church in Russia was already enduring at that time.

The Holy Spirit helped Watchman Nee and many others realize that a Chinese-style church movement was needed. An indigenous movement that blended into Chinese culture and didn't rely on ecclesiastical buildings with pointed steeples, choirs, costumed clergy, denominations, Anglo-Saxon liturgies, foreign music, pews, religious careerism, seminaries, stained glass windows, and Western doctrines or theologies.

The result was a series of meetings that gave birth to the Chinese house church movement. Nee's teaching notes and lectures were transcribed and eventually published in several obscure books, including *The Normal Christian Church Life*, which is still available in the USA.[4] Although Watchman Nee died a martyr in a

Communist prison, millions have since found Christ through the movements he helped launch.

More Than a Last Days Survival Plan

The Chinese house church revival is much more than a "return to the catacombs" survival plan. Of course, it is strong protection against persecution from antichrist, but it also serves the Gospel mandate for evangelism, multiplication, renewal and outreach. It is the logical outgrowth of a belief system that is focused on the soon return of Christ.

The house church movement has become a mighty engine for delivering the message of Christ's soon return to the Chinese people — and its spreading to the rest of Asia as well. Often unconsciously (and sometimes deliberately!) the house churches follow the Bible patterns. Group behavior imitates the first century churches in four areas:

FIRST, HOUSE CHURCHES PRACTICE THE PRIESTHOOD OF ALL BELIEVERS. Meeting in open sessions, house church believers fulfill Paul's exhortation in 1 Corinthians 14:26. Everyone is expected to share a song, a testimony, an exhortation, or a teaching. Communion and other liturgies are not reserved for professionals. The Holy Spirit is allowed to lead the worship. Personal needs are openly shared and prayed for by the group. Reports of deliverance, healings, and miracles are so common that in many places the Communists have issued orders forbidding the laying on of hands in prayer meetings! This so-called "power evangelism" through signs and wonders has been very effective in winning millions of Chinese to Christ.

SECOND, CHINESE PRACTICE THE BIBLI-

CAL ROLE OF FATHERS, FAMILIES, AND PRI-
VATE FINANCIAL RESPONSIBILITY. By centering
Church gatherings in homes and family business areas,
leadership tends to be more patriarchal and integrated
into everyday living. Chinese have not developed the
dichotomy between their family lifestyles and their
faith that is so common in America. Faith is better
integrated into the secular, work-a-day world. Families,
not government welfare or the church, are still the basic
"safety net" in Asian society. The house churches rein-
force the Biblical concepts of personal and family
responsibility for finance.

THIRD, CHINESE ARE USING THE FIVE-
FOLD MINISTRY FOR EQUIPPING THE SAINTS
TO DO THE MINISTRY. Most pastoral care is not
handled by professional clergy in China. What we
would call "lay pastors," "deacons," or "bi-vocational"
ministers here in the United States are responsible for
this ministry at the house church level. Those with the
full-time gifts travel between local church congregations (see Eph. 4:11-12). House churches may be regularly visited by these missionaries, teachers, pastors,
evangelists and prophets — but not "led" by them! The
five-fold ministries are usually practiced one-on-one or
in citywide meetings of the whole church. There are also
rare "conference" or retreat settings when cell leaders
are able to gather for fellowship and equipping. In this
way, doctrinal errors, heresies, and cultic sects are
corrected.

FOURTH, HOUSE CHURCHES SEE THE
GROWING NEED FOR PERSONAL PIETY. The
simplicity of the house churches of China foster holiness, practical love, and unity. It is almost impossible to

keep secrets. Problems are known to all. There is little in house church meetings to attract the carnally-minded, worldly-wise Christian. The small group format promotes close fellowship and mutual support. There is a strong emphasis on the practical exhortations to holiness found in Corinthians or James, and chapters like Galatians 5-6, Ephesians 4-5, and Philippians 4.

China's End-Times Gift to the Nations

China's modern-day saints and martyrs have modeled a unique lifestyle to the bride of Christ everywhere — and even to the unconverted in our secularized, watching world. For Christians on the brink of the 21st century, the persecuted church in China has much to teach us. We have much to learn. The Chinese are able to help us as post-modern Christians rediscover something we have lost — the need to share the incredible, life-changing power of the simple Gospel in the context of our everyday lifestyles. And the Chinese are doing this in a materialistic, pseudo-scientific environment extremely hostile to faith. It is the kind of anti-Christian environment increasingly challenging people of faith here in the USA. As antichrist grows stronger and stronger in the West, we will need to adopt Chinese methods of survival in order to face growing persecution.

For non-believers in Asia and around the world, the Chinese Christian Diaspora offers a unique, new source of Christ's gospel — as well as a new model for the church. More than any other nation, they are carrying Christ's torch of hope into the next century. In the end, will it be the Church that comes from the East which will complete the Great Commission? Will Chinese and other East Asian missionaries do the most to bring lasting peace to earth? The possibility is strong.

If so, what must our response be? How can we be part of God's end times move in China, and in our own personal lives and spheres of influence? Each reader of this book has an environment to reach for Christ — and a part to play. The suffering underground church has shown us the way by their passionate devotion to Christ's soon return.

[1]*Prayerline*, November 1996, Christian Aid Mission.

[2]National and International Religion Report, April 29, 1996, Volume 10, Number 10, page 1.

[3]Carl Lawrence, *The Coming Influence of China* (Gresham, OR: Vision House Publishing, Inc., 1996), p.136.

[4]Watchman Nee, *The Normal Christian Church Life* (Anaheim, CA: Living Stream Ministry, 1980).

Chapter 5

The Dragon's War on Human Rights

For we wrestle not against flesh and blood, but against principalities, against powers, against the rulers of the darkness of this age, against spiritual hosts of wickedness in the heavenly places (Eph. 6:12).

Writing this chapter takes personal courage for me! I must often travel to China, so I know firsthand how vengeful the Red Dragon's retribution can be. Yet I must speak out. No honest book on China today can avoid tackling this subject.

American Christians simply cannot understand the perverse pleasure Satan takes out of abusing, enslaving, shaming, and torturing the Chinese people. Nor can Americans understand how U.S. corporations and even government officials seem so powerless to do anything to change things. Why can't they stop looking the other way and get involved? I cannot betray my readers by skipping this chapter.

The subject of human rights has to be addressed because exposure to light is the first step for China's healing. The only way to cleanse the land of its endemic "human rights infection" is to expose it to a strong antiseptic — the cleansing of her wounds through "truth-telling."

Is Cruelty and Shame Necessary?

I realize that many Chinese leaders honestly believe that cruelty and shame are necessary evils on the road to progress — that these methods are the only way to modernize China. They don't understand the evil force behind their actions is the Red Dragon and legions of demons.

That's why Chinese Christian leaders are able to pray for their tormentors — just as Christ did from the cross, saying "forgive them for they know not what they do."

Many dedicated Communists and young nationalists who operate the Bamboo Gulag have not learned the way of love that Christ teaches. They sincerely want to erase the shame of past foreign domination, and lead the nation to prosperity. After centuries of chaos they long for the discipline and order that civil peace brings to business, education, and family. Chinese Christians understand these yearnings and share in them. That's why Chinese believers and churches have never united to work politically against the Communists or other political powers! Even though Christians are perhaps the most abused and discriminated against population in China today, they only return good for evil.

The Cosmic Source of Human Rights Abuses

Of course, neither the Communists nor any other human rulers or political parties are the ultimate source of the human rights crisis in China. They are all merely pawns in the hands of the dragon. Many of those who abuse Christians — like those who abuse children here in the United States — are themselves former victims of abuse.

So while China's politicians keep insisting that human rights violations in China are their business alone, the truth is far more sinister. The real source of such tyranny in China is cosmic. It comes from the spiritual world. It is demon forces that are abusing and oppressing China's people — spiritual forces far stronger than any political party or secret police force!

Meanwhile, Beijing's secular propagandists continue preaching the official line. "The rest of the world are hypocrites," say their spin doctors. Every time a new "Laogai" horror is revealed, they shoot back "You Americans should focus on correcting your own problems!" They cite the beatings of Mexican immigrants or Rodney King as evidence of American police brutality whenever another case of Chinese police terror is exposed.

Where Is America's Courage?

After years of painful experience dealing with the Chinese, the U.S. State Department has been especially vulnerable to this kind of guilt-tripping propaganda war. American firms sell Chinese secret police much of their technology and weapons. President Bill Clinton naively took the bait when he first assumed office and is now hooked. After he de-linked trade relations from China's massive violations of universal human rights treaties, he found the U.S. no longer had any leverage to restrain the Chinese or negotiate. Only the Pacific Fleet and our atomic arsenal are left to curb the Chinese — dangerous weapons which aren't much use in peace time to influence civilian affairs.

Meanwhile, our "engagement through trade" policy looks the other way when sadistic secret police haul away the innocent — leaving the goon squads free to increase their imprisonment, execution rates, and torture. Almost daily, new reports of police attacks on Chinese Christians are revealed — often including deaths and permanent injuries.

Why Governments Remain Silent

Although most diplomats agree privately that China is among the worst violators of human rights in the world today, Beijing has managed to cower them into silence. There are few governments or UN agencies left that have the courage or willpower to hold the hardline Stalinists of China accountable for their crimes against humanity.

"Outsiders have no business coming into China and being concerned about our children, our religious minorities, our political prisoners, or our women," argue the propagandists. Even the United Nations backs down when the Chinese use this defense. Many of the former non-aligned nations join this conspiracy of silence because their own human rights records are so bad. This leaves innocent victims of government-sponsored terror without a human advocate inside or outside

China. Thus religious believers and their families have little legal recourse in the Chinese justice system. China's state-controlled media does not expose police abuses of Christians.

No wonder the prisons and torture chambers of China have become temples of prayer to the Living God — many innocent Christians suffer in them daily, and their blood cries out to heaven. Christians around the world need to be praying daily for prisoners of conscience in China.

Why Christians Care about Human Rights

Not surprisingly, it is Christians inside and outside China who continue to care most about human suffering wherever it occurs. This is because Jesus Christ cares — and commands his followers to care. The hungry, the orphaned, the sick, prisoners, and widows are our first line of ministry. "Whatever you do to the least of my brethren," Christ said, "you do to me" (Matt. 25:37-40).

So for the Christian, Chinese human rights are not a political issue. That's what Marx and Lenin didn't understand — and what the Maoists still don't understand about Christians. We know that sooner or later, communism in China will fall from power just as every other dynasty has. But human rights will still be a Christian concern no matter what human government rules.

The demise of communism will not mean that the dragon's war on Chinese humanity will end! Marxist/ Leninism was merely a very convenient, politically correct garment for the dragon to take on in the 20th century. It was like the snake's skin in the Garden of Eden. Or like this year's pop fashion — good for one season only. Communism in China will be discarded when Satan has no more use for it. That may even be what is actually happening in Hong Kong now.

"Communism will not take over capitalist Hong Kong," jokes Chinese missionary Freddy Sun of Christian Aid with a hearty laugh, "but capitalist Hong Kong will take over Communist China!" (Freddy and Dorothy, like many Chinese missionaries, spent years in Communist labor camps and prisons. Yet they are soft-spoken and forgiving about their former tormentors.)

Many believe he is right. However, even if true, it's not likely to reduce the dragon's chokehold on the neck of the Chinese. A free market does not make a free people. In fact, it opens doors for the more respectable demons of avarice, greed and lust to tempt believers! So for the Chinese, the present Communist oppression is just another chapter in 3,000 years of cruel tyranny. Past dictators also ruled capitalist or fascist economies. Human rights abuses were just as frequent then as they are today.

Who's Behind Chinese Human Rights Abuses?

The parade of dictators in China didn't begin with Mao Tse Tung in 1945! Nor even with the First Qin in 221 B.C. China has always had more than its share of Genghis Khans, Manchus, and lesser characters like Deng Xiaoping. Though he masterminded the current economic reform, he also ordered tanks to roll over students in Tiananmen Square! Deng oversees the world's largest secret police force, a network of informers that extends all the way down to every block and apartment building.

The dragon's abuse of humanity dates all the way

back to the very roots of Chinese civilization. There has never been democracy or freedom in China. The bondage of the Han, the Cantonese, the Hunan and other Chinese nations has always been primarily spiritual rather than physical or political.

The dragon is the real tyrant. Human dictators like Hitler, Mao, Stalin, and even Sadam Hussein are only his pawns. In his or her heart, every thinking Chinese knows that there is a power behind the powers that oppress the land. You sense it in Beijing at the Temple of Heaven or strolling on the Great Wall.

Folk Festivals Honor the Dragon

The proof of this is repeated each year during the Lunar Festival. Chinese dutifully sweep out their houses and hang long, blood-red signs on the doorposts. These scrolls of fiery poster paper vividly recall images of the Jews applying blood on their door-frames at Passover. In fact, the Lunar New Year has been called Chinese Passover.

Just as the Jews go to the table for their seder meal, the whole Chinese family gathers inside to eat a festive banquet. After a splendid feast, something akin to our Thanksgiving, the Chinese must remain indoors till dawn.

At sunrise, they emerge and ceremonially congratulate each other — grateful for their "good luck" at not being eaten by the dragon during the night! According to Wright Doyle of the China Institute, this Chinese "passover" ritual mimics the Bible, but honors the real ruling spirit of China.

To understand modern Chinese culture, you must understand that dragon worship is real. He still rules.

The dragon's icon is everywhere you go. Dragon idols coil from cornices and pillars of the most modern buildings. Even in the lobby of Taipei's Grand Hotel, this ferocious image looms overhead on the ceiling — transforming what should simply be a modern hotel into a temple as ancient as Han themselves.

The Real Ruler of China

Not even the Communists, with their secularistic worship of Britain's 19th century scientific materialism, can rid themselves of this popular image. It's on a thousand socialist products from airline fuselages to tea cups. Why, if the dragon is only superstition, do even Marxists honor him?

This Antichrist image cleverly personifies the god of all things Chinese admire most. He is the ultimate ruling spirit — accommodating to his adversaries, yet relentlessly aggressive. He is urbane and witty, an evolving cross-cultural demon who never forsakes his dedication to Chinese racism and roots. He is seemingly invincible and all-powerful, maintaining superiority and control. He is adaptive to environmental changes, tenacious, ever-working, and always seems victorious in the end.

The Chinese Dragon can be generous to his vanquished subjects but spiteful and vengeful to his enemies. Terror and deprivation are his favorite weapons of control — and so he is able to easily rule the covetous, cowardly, and greedy. No wonder the history of China sometimes reads like a catalog of human rights violations!

The dragon is a master of spiritual bondage and holds his greedy, addicted worshippers with moral fetters. Fear is the buckle on these spiritual restraints, and it works on the avaricious best of all. Jealousy and greed and the twin iniquities the dragon has used to bind the Chinese — and that's why only love can release them!

The Dragon as Dracula

The Red Dragon is really a monster come alive, but worshipped instead of slain. In the West, writes Jim Ward, the dragon symbolizes the terrible — something to be defeated or conquered. "In the East however, the dragon is a symbol of transformation, and its mystery and power are revered. It can make itself large or small, powerful or meek, exceptional or ordinary; it can take the form of animals, rocks, even human beings. Because they are always changing, dragons are impossible to predict or measure; hence our Western, scientific world is essentially unable to perceive them. If I wanted to encounter dragons, I knew I would have to leave behind all I had learned in college and in church, travel through the blank spaces, and learn to see with Eastern eyes."[1]

In Chinese mythology, the dragon overcomes and subdues the phoenix. Is it coincidence that his legendary enemy, like Christ, rises from the dead? Of course not, the Red Dragon is the spirit of antichrist and his enemy is the Lord Jesus.

That great snake, the dragon of Revelation 12:7-9, is the biblical "strongman" behind a legion of sadistic spirits that have made the Chinese people their spiritual bondslaves. The Chinese people are mere toys for their cruel contests. These sports are acted out upon the Chinese with verbal and physical abuse. Violence and death are the last play in the game.

No believer should underestimate the death-dealing power of the antichrist. Jim Ward likens the Great Dragon to the Vampire legend of Count Dracula — which literally means Count Dragon. "The dark side of the dragon, and polar opposite of a bodhisattva, Dracula sucks the life-blood of his victims in order that he may live forever, and damns them to share his living death."[2]

Knowing that his days are numbered, the Chinese Dragon hates humanity. No wonder he literally seeks the death of as many Chinese as he can consume. The dragon will go down in flames, but not without taking billions of Chinese souls with him!

Why Christians Cannot Remain Silent

That's why Christians everywhere — even patriotic Chinese believers living under the dragon — don't remain inactive in the face of human rights violations. Christians may not be able to speak out prophetically in China today, but they are still the primary mercy corps healing the wounds of the dragon. That's why the Church is growing everywhere, bearing the light of Christ into the darkness.

If China had freedom of speech and press, Christians would instinctively speak out with the love that Christ instills in them for the suffering. Christians know the wellspring of persecution is not the Communists or the government — Lucifer is the ultimate master of deceit. He is behind every violation of human rights in China. Lucifer, who should be bearing the light of God's glory, is today using his media powers to obscure that glory and deceive the Chinese people.

He continually dispatches lying spirits — master

Two decades after his death bloody dictator
Mao Tse Tung still watches over the Communist empire.

Underground Christian meetings.

Dragon architecture dominates . . .

. . . everything in Asia.

Joseph Lam with
Mother Teresa in
Calcutta.

Joseph Lam
holding one
of the
precious
little ones
behind the
Bamboo
Curtain.

The Chinese military is rapidly advancing into the 21st century.

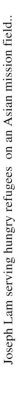

This is the face of Chinese oppression.

Joseph Lam serving hungry refugees on an Asian mission field..

The price of Christian worship in China.

The incidents of firing squad executions are on the rise in China. Communist leaders are "flexing their muscles" to achieve more prestige and power in the new regime after Deng Xiaoping's death.

China right now is suffering the greatest attack of persecution and torture at the hands of the Communists since the Tiananmen Square massacre.

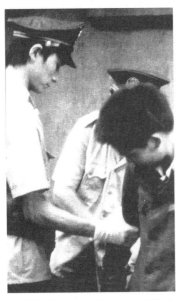

Life for an underground Christian means living with the threat of arrest for themselves or their families every hour of every day, for their faith in Christ.

Tiananmen Square victims.

propagandists — to confuse the outside world about his Chinese kingdom. These lying spirits work on many different levels to misrepresent the truth about China in the West. Some even pose as clergy. Other demons speak through respectable channels such as diplomats, doctors, journalists, and educators.

Christ told us that only the blinding spotlight of truth will set the Chinese free (John 8:32). The most important action the rest of the Christian world can do to support the Chinese today is to preach the truth of the gospel.

The moral epidemic in China is the same disease destroying the United States and western culture. Sin rules! Social problems in China and the United States are merely extensions of our personal rebellion against God. This is why the Chinese have a human rights crisis — and why it will only grow worse unless the light of the Gospel is allowed to freely shine.

China and the Big Lie

The dragon has successfully used the Communists and their "big lie" propaganda technology to mask the truth for five decades. Wherever you go in the world's of education, government, media, and religion you will hear the same advice.

"Wait and things will get better," the pundits chant in near perfect unity. But things never really get better. Every day longer the dragon holds power in China, hundreds of thousands of Chinese souls go to the eternal flames of hell without hearing the gospel.

"Patience is all we ask from the United States," say the demon-inspired apologists for Beijing. But the dragon has no intention of loosening his grip on the

Chinese without divine intervention. The present "waiting game" merely buys him additional time to destroy more souls.

That's why he doesn't fear unwinnable wars, endless revolutions, failed economic and social schemes or anything else which costs Chinese lives. The death toll from the failed experiment in Chinese communism exceeds all the other atrocities of 20th century combined.

The March of Death Continues

Yet Satan continues to promote population control through abortion in China. Endless wars of liberation grind on long after Mao's death from Africa to Afghanistan. Party purges and deadly development and social programs spin out of control. The dragon cares not — loss of life is always a victory to him.

It is true that big, public massacres like the Great Cultural Revolution or Tiananmen Square usually occur only once every decade. After the blood is mopped up, the dragon's death squads always say they've learned — and this will be the last time. Meanwhile, the grinding degradation of the Chinese people goes on day after endless day. Just because it isn't always a hideous mass-murder or government-made famine, that doesn't mean the persecution is not violent.

Millions upon millions of times every hour Satan torments the stoic Chinese Christians with such "small scale" violence. This persecution is more subtle — deprivation of food and income, interrogations, registrations, regulations, and verbal abuse. Satan doesn't just want the death of the Chinese people, he wants to make their lives as miserable as he can while they live.

That's why the dragon will promise anything and do anything if we Christians in the free world will only leave him and his demons alone. He always needs a cloak of dark silence covering up his crimes against the innocent. That's why he trades favors with foreign business leaders, diplomats, media persons, missionaries and presidents. He must quiet those who know the truth — and keep them quiet.

The dragon even blackmails and speaks through apostate clergy in the West. Some Chinese believers, fearing retribution against their families, are being used this way as well. They work for Satan by begging the Church overseas to stop broadcasting the gospel of liberty and bearing the light of Christ into China!

But we cannot stop. Isaiah predicted that Christ would proclaim liberty to the captives — and Christ stood in the synagogue and affirmed that this was indeed His messianic mission to the world. On the first Ascension Day, he transferred His mission to His church. As much as we might desire friendship and peace with all men, we cannot deny our Lord. We must proclaim liberty to the Chinese and all other nations. We simply cannot remain silent and still be Christians.

Documenting Human Rights Violations in China

It is not the purpose of this book to re-tell horror stories of state-sanctioned atrocities and sadism in China today. This grisly task is being handled by Asia Rights Watch, Amnesty International, Christian Solidarity International, plus a number of non-profit information services like Compass and the now-defunct News Network International. Even the State Department, the president, and the United Nations have opened offices to handle reports of human rights abuses in China. In addition, every Chinese church and mission society has filing cabinets full of reports on the growing number of martyred and missing Christians.

Persecution Is on the Increase

Since the Tiananmen Square massacre, the drumbeat of this new wave of persecution against innocent believers has increased significantly. Statistics on the current "strike hard" wave of persecution, which really began in 1994, are hard to find. It is safe to say that hundreds, sometimes thousands of raids are being made on houses churches every month. Despite censorship, there are almost weekly reports of deaths and life-threatening injuries to pastors and leaders.

Daily reports are arriving from all over China which confirm what the United Nations says about the current increase in persecution:

> Since 1992, the policy of repression pursued by the Chinese authorities against both Protestant and Catholic churches outside official structures is said to have taken on new dimensions, including the resumption of sentencing by administrative decree, the transfer of prisoners from judicial to administrative detention, the repeated use of torture and continual reaffirmation by the authorities of their determination to put an end to 'illegal' religious activities.[3]

Pedro Moreno of the Rutherford Institute, writing in the authoritative *Handbook on Religious Liberty*

Around the World (1996 Edition) classifies China and Tibet as among the "frequent" and "serious" violators of international conventions on religious rights.[4]

Moreno says that while the Chinese constitution actually guarantees religious freedom, these rights are voided through administrative decrees. The documents are issued by the Chinese Communist party and enforced through the Public Security Bureau Police. Corrupt local police spies and a provincial system of Religious Affairs Bureaus are used to identify and target Christians for persecution by the "thought police."

"China requires all religious organizations to join state-controlled churches," reports Moreno, "thereby restricting their activities. Those who fail to register, or criticize the government, face imprisonment, torture and/or execution. There is further suppression in Tibet, which is now controlled by China, and any practice of faith is severely restricted."[5]

China Watch: Combating Terror with Prayer

So what should Christians around the world do to respond to the suffering in China? Over 80 percent of the top Church leaders in Hong Kong whom we surveyed for this book say prayer is their greatest need — and they really mean it.

Since human rights abuse in China are basically a spiritual problem, it requires a spiritual solution. Indeed, because of government xenophobia, traditional protests and boycotts often backfire on the very Chinese believers one seeks to help.

This doesn't mean that selective boycotts, demonstrations, diplomacy, exchange visits, letter-writing campaigns, mercy missions, protests, visitations, and even publicity should not be used. Two cautions are required:

First, such actions need to be approved and initiated by Chinese Christian leaders. They have to suffer the consequences and retribution. If local Chinese pastors are supporting some kind of social action or protest, then it is probably the right time for a public witness. Such efforts help follow-up their prayers, and the prayers of the international Christian community for China.

Which leads to the second caution. All action must be conceived and born from the womb of prayer. It must be prayer first. Prayer foremost. Prayer always.

Second Corinthians 4:9-10 explains that the weapons of our warfare are not carnal. We are warned not to war according to the flesh — using human wisdom or power politics. Ephesians 6 lays down the rules for warfare praying against human rights abuses in China.

So how does one effectively "watch and pray" for the suffering churches of China? Christians in the West need to follow the news in prayer. Every article, broadcast, fax release, newsletter, or Internet item on China is a call to prayer. You can even pray-read the encyclopedia, books like Operation World and various prayer diaries and letters. Prayer walks in Chinatown and encounters with Chinese friends and strangers can be occasions for prayer.

Become a student of China and her needs. Get a big map of China and Asia for your bedroom wall. As you learn more about China and her needs, begin to locate the places and peoples you are praying for on your map. America needs a new generation of China-lovers and China-prayers.

A Generic Prayer List for Human Rights

Chinese house church leaders outline at least 14 generic areas of concern for intercession. You may use this Human Rights Prayer List anytime as a guide spiritual warfare against the dragon.

(1) FREEDOM OF ASSEMBLY — Pray that registered and unregistered congregations will be able to freely meet without restrictions. Pray that Christians will be released from the "three designate" regulations; restrictions that allow them to meet only at designated times, places, and under government approved clergy. Pray for freedom to plan their own programs, to do evangelism and teach from the Bible freely. Pray that Sunday schools will be allowed to reopen, and subject matter of sermons and Bible study will be unrestricted. Pray that Christian congregations and student groups will be allowed to gather publicly for all Christian holidays — not just Christmas and Easter celebrations. Pray that evangelistic crusades and Bible teaching conferences will be permitted. Pray that open air evangelism will again be permitted in parks and public places.

(2) FREEDOM FOR BIBLE PUBLICATION AND DISTRIBUTION — Pray that unlimited amounts of Bibles, hymnals, prayer books, and other literature will be published and distributed through the normal book trade including bookshops, booktables, bookstalls and libraries. Pray that Bibles will become widely available again to the public through itinerant colporteurs and traveling evangelists.

(3) FREEDOM FROM CENSORSHIP — Pray that the strict censorship of Christian events, programs, and publications will be lifted at every level.

(4) FREEDOM FROM PARTY AND GOVERN-

MENT CONTROL — Pray for political parties and government leaders according to 1 Timothy 2:1-2 that constitutional guarantees of religious freedom will be protected. Pray that efforts to control and use Christian groups through United Front networks, Religious Affairs Bureaus, and patriotic religious organizations will be abandoned.

(5) FREEDOM FOR THE FAMILY — Pray for the freedom to marry and raise families according to Bible principles, including the right to a Christian education for children.

(6) FREEDOM FOR HONG KONG AND OTHER GATEWAY CITIES — Pray for the transition of Hong Kong to Chinese sovereignty, a process that is scheduled to take 50 years, until 2047. Pray that the basic law protecting religious freedom will be defended, enforced and respected. Pray that all religious freedoms including evangelism and outreach will be protected and expand naturally into all of China. Pray that the door to China will swing open rather than closed for the Gospel.

(7) FREEDOM FOR LAY PERSONS — Pray that lay Christians will be "victors not victims" of Satanic oppression according to Matthew 16:19, and that bi-vocational ministries will be recognized. Pray for freedom to visit hospitals and public institutions as lay and full-time chaplains.

(8) FREEDOM FOR LEADERSHIP TRAINING — Pray that Bible schools and seminaries in Hong Kong and throughout China will produce a new generation of trained missionaries and pastors. Pray for the development of Bible schools to train thousands of church planters and evangelists who will be able to complete

the Great Commission in China and nearby countries. Pray for pastors who will be able to shepherd the flock, lead a new generation of Christian young people, and protect the Church from error, heresy, and the sins of maturing and prospering congregations.

(9) FREEDOM FOR MISSIONS — Itinerant ministries, including the five-fold ministries, need freedom to travel and conduct meetings without restrictions. This includes preachers, teachers and musicians. Also, Christian groups should be allowed to again open ministries to alcoholics, addicts, children, homeless, the mentally ill and refugees. Finally, pray that Chinese Christians will be allowed to reopen clinics, hospitals, orphanages, schools, and other institutions and raise public funds to operate.

(10) FREEDOM FROM PERSECUTORS — Pray for the Public Security Bureau Police, provincial Religious Affairs Bureau chiefs, local police, and local party officials. Pray that many more of them will be converted as Paul was and turned from persecutors to promoters of Christ and His church. Pray that their hearts will be tender toward the witness of the men and women they arrest and persecute, and that they will show mercy to the innocent.

(11) FREEDOM OF PRESS AND MEDIA — Pray that Christian newspapers, magazines, radio, TV, and video products will again be published without government control or restriction.

(12) FREEDOM FOR PRISON MINISTRIES — Pray for the prisoners according to Hebrews 13:3 that they will be victors and not victims of their jailers and tormentors. Pray that they will lead many of their jailers and fellow prisoners to Christ, as Paul and Barnabas did

in Philippi and Rome. Pray that they will learn much about the Lord during their trauma and emerge from jail as stronger leaders. Pray for those who are being tortured, raped, or abused that angels will protect and comfort them.

(13) FREEDOM FOR SLAVE LABORERS — Pray for Christians accused of minor public order and counter-revolutionary offenses who are being held without charge in the Chinese "Laogai" gulag. Pray for Christians who are separated from family and undergoing "re-education through labor" in these prison factories and work camps. Pray that they will be used to bring many fellow prisoners to Christ and that labor camps will be used to train missionaries. Pray for safety in dangerous working conditions, handling radioactive and carcinogenic chemicals. Pray for those manufacturing war supplies, weapons, or products that are offensive to their conscience.

(14) FREEDOM OF SPEECH — Pray for the protection of itinerant evangelists, teachers, and preachers. Pray that wide open doors will be given for them to proclaim the gospel. Pray that they will be safe from discovery by police spies and for strength and health when they are arrested and tortured.

(15) FREEDOM FOR WOMEN, BABIES, AND THE INFIRM — Pray for Christian mothers who become pregnant after having the one child they are allowed by law under China's population control program. Pray that they and their babies will be saved from forced abortions. Pray for deliverance of babies from selective sex abortion. Pray for the murders to stop; for salvation of babies, the elderly, the infirm, and prisoners who are killed for cannibalism or the harvest of organs

and body tissue. Pray for the sanctity of human life to be restored in Chinese society.

The Dragon and Religious Freedom

I have focused mostly in this chapter on the dragon's hatred of universal human rights — denying them is the key that locks the chains on his Chinese slaves. But there is another set of rights he hates even more. Those are the rights that give birth to human rights and freedom. The mother of all freedoms is freedom of worship and religion. The dragon hates freedom of religion more than any other liberty. In our next chapter, we will explore the deadly myth of China's underground church success — and why religious freedom must come.

[1]Jim Ward, *The Great Dragon's Fleas* (Berkeley, CA: Celestial Arts, 1993), page XI.

[2]Ibid., page 42

[3]November 25, 1993, "Letter from the Special Rapporteur to the Government of China," in United Nations: Economic and Social Council, Implementation of the Declaration on the Elimination of All Forms of Intolerance and of Discrimination Based on Religion and Belief, E/CN.4/1994/79 (20 January 1994):38.

[4]"Handbook on Religious Liberty Around the World," edited by Pedro C. Moreno, Rutherford Institute, 1996, page 49,

[5]Ibid.

Chapter 6

The Dragon and the Myth of the Underground Church

And they cried with a loud voice, saying "How long, Oh lord, holy and true, until you judge and avenge our blood on those who dwell on the earth? (Rev. 6:10).

Just how much Chinese blood must still be spilt in order to plant the kingdom of God in the Middle Kingdom? To bring "liberty to the captives" and proclaim that "the day of the Lord has come" to China? Not since the days of Emperor Nero has any human government so resisted the growth of the Church. The blood of China's martyrs flows like a never-ending stream before the throne of God.

Yet no one can deny that the growing churches of China are thriving in spite of their bloodthirsty opposition. Since the dragon forced the true Church underground, it has multiplied at least 30-fold. (Many insist that it has grown much more than that.)

Even in Hong Kong, revival broke out on the eve of the Communist takeover. The churches are packed in anticipation of persecution! The number of congregations has grown from 800 to 1,200 in less than three years. Meanwhile, Chinese lay believers are going underground to form "cell churches" in their homes and train a new layer of shadow leadership — a sure sign of even more growth to come.

Is Persecution Always Good?

But is this persecution always good for the Church? You would think so from the way many western preachers and writers have romanticized the martyrs of China. Sometimes it seems they almost relish the terror — as if somehow it is a good thing!

"Maybe we need some persecution like that in America," say these approving cynics with a certain glee. "That would purify the Church in the States and get us moving again!"

However, I can't believe anyone would say such things if they could visit the underground church as I have. This persecution is as evil and vile as any in history. Anyone who reads the macabre daily reports of what is happening in China today will have a hard time not getting sick to the stomach.

A New Wave of Terror

For example, just as we were starting this chapter, the telecopier machine rang. It was yet another overseas fax from Hong Kong, confirming what we already know from scores of other reports. The current persecution of the underground church is spreading throughout all the provinces of China. Since 1949 persecution has been steady, but there are also tidal waves of terror. One such "new phase" of persecution is underway now. Fearing another Tiananmen Square, the hardliners have ordered the police to renew their sadistic attacks on innocent Christians, and especially upon the house churches.

Yet, characteristically, the Chinese look upon this as a time of blessing! "This is a special time," writes one Hong Kong pastor, "the Lord is visiting the Chinese church. Some are seeing more converts in one week than they have seen in decades.

"But our brothers and sisters in China are still suffering. This past week in Henan the Communist police beat to death one of the young preachers (a sister) who works with us. In another area, Northeast China, they took five into the station and poured scalding water over them until their skin began to peel, and then beat them until their front teeth came out.

"They then mocked them and challenged them to praise the Lord as they had been doing in church when they were arrested. The brothers began to sing beautiful songs of praise until it filled the police station. These wicked men were so ashamed of what they had done when they saw the presence of the Lord in these young preachers that they released them all. This just happened a few days ago."

Incidents like this occur daily all over China, but with every atrocity committed, the body of Christ becomes stronger.

Effectiveness of Persecution

As always, God is bringing forth beauty from ashes. While the victorious testimonies of the suffering Chinese are encouraging — they must not seduce us into complacency. We need to share their pain and repent of our lack of love toward their needs.

God's word says "When one member of the body suffers, we all suffer" (1 Cor. 12:26). We are wounded by every wound the Antichrist inflicts on the church in China. American believers need to realize that they are impacted daily by what is happening today in China, and will be for years to come.

The USA and China are locked in a desperate economic embrace. Depending on how we react, it will become an embrace of death or life for both our cultures. What happens to the Chinese people and the churches of China in the next few years is going to affect the way we live, what we wear, and even how we eat. The destiny of China and the United States are intertwined.

Because of this special relationship that is developing between the United States and China, we have opportunities to interact with the Chinese at many levels. With these opportunities comes the obligation to speak out in defense of those who cannot defend themselves.

Our president and State Department in Washington have put our economic prosperity ahead of universal human rights for too long. God hears the prayers of the suffering Chinese church in the Bamboo Gulag, and divine judgment will fall on the USA if we don't do more to support the persecuted churches.

China Will Benefit from a Free Church

Just imagine what a powerhouse for end-times evangelism and development the Chinese could be if they allowed Christians to be free. What if their energy, entrepreneurism, and love were released to bless the nations of the world rather than foster economic exploitation, terrorism, and war?

If the churches of China were again allowed to support indigenous missionaries, it would change the whole face of Asia. If the government took a hands-off approach — and allowed Demetrius instead of Diotrephes to lead the Chinese Church — imagine what powerful senders they would become! Not only would Chinese evangelists reach every village and hamlet in their own land, but they will go on to all of Central Asia and the Middle East.

While persecution is intense now, it is quite likely that the doors and windows of religious freedom will open and shut several times between now and Armageddon. The dragon is going to be pre-occupied and we need to be ready to step into "windows of opportunity" as they appear.

The Blessings of Religious Freedom

The blessings of religious freedom would benefit China and the churches of China in many ways. We need to pray and work for freedoms like these to be restored in the 21st century:

(1) Itinerant preachers and Bible teachers could travel again. Nothing is more needed right now. With upwards of 20,000 unregistered house churches, there is a great need for gifted evangelism and Bible teaching. In the short term, this need can only be met through

circuit-riding preachers like the Wesleyan Methodists who rode our western frontiers on horseback.

(2) Children would be healed, and the family restored. Today in the former USSR, much of the country is ruled by Mafia-style mobs of gangsters. Three generations of atheistic brainwashing left the country without a moral code. Millions of Russians can no longer discern right from wrong. The same thing is happening in China today. China is raising a new generation of self-centered young criminals. Children and youth are growing up with no belief other than "might makes right" and "get rich quick!"

After re-starting Sunday schools and Christian education, the Chinese church needs to birth indigenous versions of movements like "Promise Keepers" to re-store concepts of Christian fatherhood, husbandry, and marriage. The same forces that have perverted gender relationships in the West are taking over in Asia — and with good reason. Women have been exploited and abused for thousands of years all across Asia. Satan can build a strong case for secular feminism in Asia, with the same devastating results that have wrecked families and children here.

So the Chinese are in danger of losing their family structure, too. AIDS is on the increase as promiscuity and the sexual revolution creeps across the landscape. Biblical teaching is needed to help men and women understand their God-given roles in the Christian family and society.

Each nation and society has it's own endemic problems — which are compounded by 19th century secular materialism. Chinese men, women, children, youth, and elderly all face unique social challenges that need to be addressed with Bible answers. The Chinese will develop their own movements to provide biblical solutions, of course. But in order to do so, they have to have the freedom to organize and release their natural missionary entrepreneurism.

(3) Churches could again start up orphanages, schools, hospitals, and other much-needed institutions. Beginning with Bible schools and seminaries, religious freedom would allow the Church to rebuild a network of much-needed institutions. In these institutions, the Chinese will be able to cultivate Christian ethics, piety, and model Christian lifestyles for modern China.

In such institutions, the Holy Spirit could be allowed to freely develop the devotional lives and piety of the Chinese races. Who can possibly imagine what kind of Christian citizen will develop if the Holy Spirit is allowed full freedom to develop Chinese believers? How many more Billy Grahams and Watchman Nees are latent in the Chinese church?

Privately operated Christian orphanages and schools are needed to provide choice and raise the overall standards of child-care and education throughout China — not to speak of rural and slum areas still lacking adequate institutions. China's state monopoly on education helps the dragon maintain political control, but it blocks millions of children from developing their minds and spirits.

(4) Media networks could be established. Christian publishing of Bibles and books, as well as educational curriculum are just the beginning of what China needs now. Distribution and retailing networks must be established for all kinds of Christian books, tapes, and products. Plus, to cover all of China, hundreds of

Christian radio and TV stations are needed to help fill the empty airwaves. Chinese Christian satellite networks could feed and produce religious programs to all of Asia as well as the China mainland. China's publishing houses could produce Christian literature for export to the world as well as the huge domestic market.

(5) International fellowship could be restored. The Church knows no national boundaries of course. It is above man-made cultural and political barriers such as the 20th century nation-states established by the former colonial powers. Christians in China have much to give the rest of the world — and other nationalities have much to share with China. Full religious freedom would provide for the exchange of emergency relief, finances, materials and supplies, mentors, teachers, technology, and theology.

(6) Christian civics and vocations could flourish. Once separated from political control, Christians in China will be freer to apply biblical ideals of justice and truth to education, law, government, medicine, the military, and even politics. Now, Chinese Christians are prohibited from making a contribution to almost every important area of debate and development in China. The ministry of reconciliation which follows the Church wherever it goes is much needed in China. Having Godly perspectives on matters of national concern will help China develop the common decency it needs to more peacefully face the moral choices of the 21st century.

(7) Great Commission mission agencies could be established. This will be the most important benefit of religious freedom in China. The Chinese are the greatest untapped source of natural missionaries in the world.

They have already crossed most of the cultural and political barriers in Asia through immigration, and are in positions to establish the next generation of missionary orders. Energetic, industrious, and steeled in the flames of persecution, they understand the sacrifices necessary to complete the work of Christ's Great Commission in Asia. Chinese ministries could bless the world. Religious freedom in China would unleash the Chinese churches to become a blessing and benefit to all the nations of Asia.

Why persecution Is Increasing

It is exactly this fear of a free, Spirit-filled Chinese church that keeps the dragon motivated to continue the present campaign of terror and murder. His attempts to provide a secular substitute for the church have failed. The dragon has used the utopian promises of Marxism in an attempt to create a human substitute for the provisions of the Lord through His Holy Spirit and the Church. He seeks to provide the blessings of God by purely human means. Today, Chinese at every level of society have lost faith in Lenin, Mao and Marx. They know it has failed but they don't know why.

Chinese Christians do. Marxism is man's feeble attempt to usurp the place of his loving Creator. No wonder it fails every time. Instead of love, it is motivated by fear and hate. Instead of peace, it supplies violence. Instead of hope, it brings despair.

THE POWER OF LOVE — That is what confounds police spies. When the dragon's agents infiltrate the Christian community, they discover a fellowship of love and unity. Instead of intrigue and rule by calculated terror, suspense, and uncertainty — Christians depend on open communication and truth-telling. This radical love is one of the most important secrets of fellowship in the underground churches. It is something Chinese society needs and something which the dragon, of course, can never supply.

THE POWER OF PURITY — Christian fellowship in the true church of China is also based on righteousness and unity in faith and practice. It is not the political alliance or united front demanded of churches by the Three Self Patriotic movement. Holiness is so important that real Christian pastors are quite willing to endure long years in labor camps rather than join what they consider to be an apostate movement. The dragon cannot understand this. Prison, torture, and even death is preferred to compromise.

THE POWER OF THE HOLY SPIRIT — There is also the radical power of the Lord. Miracles, healings, wondrous provision, and the gifts of the Holy Spirit are spreading like a grass fire in August. In every province of China, Communist party newspapers report the growing power of this "superstition" of Jesus Christ.

These qualities of love, purity, and power are extremely attractive to the Chinese — even to local Communist party cadre. It is dangerous to assign spies and police to infiltrate a Christian gathering because so many are converted! Many cadres become believers once they get to know the Lord of the Christians they persecute. That's why party directives frequently complain that growing numbers of party members are secretly attracted to "superstitions" such as Christianity.

Churches as a Political Threat

Christians in the USA cannot understand why the

dragon considers the churches a political threat. After all, Christians don't demonstrate, organize, vote as a block, or strike.

Why then, if the Christian churches pose no political threat to the Communists, are they persecuted? Part of this goes back to Lenin's teaching that every organization with a "people base" is to be considered as a political force. Churches are viewed as a group to be mobilized for the political ends of the party.

Since churches exist as a fellowship of love, prayer and Bible study they don't fit in with political plans.

And there is another reason. The house churches model equality between all men and women. The one-man, priestly government-style of western Christianity has yielded to the priesthood of all believers in China. Most congregations are small and governed by an informally elected eldership of peers. Christians submit one to another easily without threat or force.

This is almost "democratic" — and that is the greatest political fear of the current generation of Chinese leadership. Since the Tiananmen Square massacre, democracy has been branded as an unworkable, foreign ideal. The dragon insists that it is unsuited to the problems of governing modern China. Many Communist leaders, in particular, are alarmed by similar church movements in eastern Europe — movements which gave birth to democracies which voted out Marxism.

There has never been a true separation of state and religion in Chinese history. Although Christians are inactive in politics and no direct threat to the government — it is precisely this "inactivity" that scares the dragon and his Communist front.

Christians follow their Lord, who taught that His

kingdom is not of this world. Although Chinese Christians are excellent workers and model citizens, their loyalty is to a power higher than the state. They measure party propaganda against eternal verities. For this reason, their actions are misrepresented to the people. Christians are deliberately misunderstood and often persecuted without mercy.

Should the World Stand by Silently?

Some political leaders — and even church leaders in the West — feel that what happens in Chinese torture chambers should be no concern to the rest of the world. We should just buy cheap goods off the Chinese, sell them weapons and technology — and not ask any questions about slave labor camps or human rights. In fact, this is exactly what the dragon is counting on to keep his people in power!

Harry Wu, author of *Laogai: The Chinese Gulag*, says "The Chinese are operating on several assumptions: that people are more interested in their own economic development than in freedom and democracy, that the party can remain in power even though communism has failed, that the United States and the rest of the industrialized world will pursue economic gain at the expense of human rights in China, and that China can expand its military without significant resistance from the United States."[1]

A Christian Response

I have hope — hope in America and American values. I believe that we as a nation must challenge the Chinese to change. However, whatever the world does, we as Christians cannot share the position Harry Wu says America is taking — not if we are to remain true to

Christ. He loves the Chinese people and the Chinese church. He loved them so much that he died for them. So we must reflect that love as well. What then should be done in a practical way to help the suffering saints of China? To help bring religious freedom to modern China?

First, we must pray. Every day and every time we intercede we must remember the Chinese. From our pulpits and in our private prayers, China must always be on our lips. The Bible says we need to "remember those who are in bonds." China qualifies. It is an entire nation in bondage.

God will hear and answer our prayers, just as he heard the prayer of the early Church for Peter in prison. If we do, the day will soon come when we will go to answer a knock on the door — and we will find a free Chinese church knocking. I believe. I have hope that things will change in China. That they must change.

I cannot stop China's march to Armageddon, but I can help save some of these souls. I can help the suffering church in China. Prayer is the first step.

This prayer effort for China needs to be international and daily. It needs to be fueled with calendars, bookmarks, bumper stickers, buttons, prayer letters, and daily radio broadcasts. We must keep the Chinese people before our spiritual eyes constantly until the "strong man is bound" and China is free. I'm suggesting a campaign to mobilize prayer for China and keep China on the front burner.

Second, we must de-mystify the martyrs. The over-glorification of Chinese suffering and the exaggeration of its benefits must not be used as an excuse to let it continue.

Just because God in His mercy has allowed the Chinese Church to go through these fires of testing, we must never mistake this for His will. What is happening to the Chinese Church is evil. It is plain, old fashioned sin. It is an abomination to the Lord. We can be certain that God will judge the Communists and the Chinese government for allowing it to continue all these years — and the Americans for standing by and letting the horror happen. At the judgment seat, Chinese persecutors will not be able to stand up and say "The dragon made me do it!" That excuse is not acceptable.

The Lord Jesus explained that exploitation and social injustice must come, but He also pronounced a curse on the person through whom evil comes.

Chinese Christians are dying because they are being true to Christ. They believe in one, holy, universal Church that is free to follow the Lord Jesus Christ. It dishonors their sacrifice for us to swallow the propaganda lies that say "Chinese Christians deserve their treatment because they are operating outside the law." No innocent Christian deserves to be victim of criminal attacks — even if those attacks are by police or political party officials.

Third, we must not exaggerate church growth statistics. Even though there has been tremendous church growth under persecution, this does not justify their tyranny — or our inaction. There is no denying that the Lord has used this persecution to purify His Chinese bride — but who knows how much larger and faster the Church will grow when it is free again? Or how fast it would have grown if there had been religious freedom in China?

Satan fears a free Christian church. We must constantly remind ourselves of how much bigger and stronger the churches of China will be after religious freedom comes.

A free church, separated from state control and apostasy, is the will of God. Christ is returning for such a Bride and He has given us the Holy Spirit in order to create such a church within us collectively. Our duty is to go along with the will of God, just as the Chinese believers have done.

Fourth, we must seek forgiveness for past sins and increase friendly contacts and tourism with China. Western Christians should accept our past guilt and ask forgiveness of the Chinese for historical sins. Reconciliation is needed. Anti-Chinese racism, discrimination, indentured labor in the USA, the opium trade, the opium wars, and colonization can never be defended. These past sins are still open wounds. They are remembered and rehearsed as if they happened yesterday — and Christians are still rightfully blamed for them!

Christ commanded us to "love our enemies" and so every attempt should be made to foster good relations — even with the hardline Communists — on a personal level. It starts with admitting where we have gone wrong. Contacts with the Three Self Patriotic movement leadership are wonderful opportunities to demonstrate the love of Christ and witness. Even though some top leaders in the TSPM are apostate, there are also many fine Christians in churches that belong to the TSPM.

I am not afraid to talk with the TSPM or China Christian Council leaders. We should seek dialogue, worship together and unite on projects we can both agree upon. Ironically, some financial grants are getting through now to TSPM institutions, even during these days of persecution! The government is allowing limited amounts of Bible publishing, Christian education and leadership training through the CCC and TSPM. I am all for going through these doors when they open!

Of course, all dialogue and joint-action must be encouraged without compromising the truth or our loyalty to Christ. Peace and justice ministries, reconciliation efforts, and exchange visits have barely been attempted with Chinese Christians or Communist cadre assigned to monitor the church — nor with the Marxists of Korea, Myanmar, or Vietnam. These are rich opportunities for us to witness for Christ.

Information exchange is also very important. A great deal of dis-information is going forth but "the truth will set men free." We need to re-gird ourselves with the belt of truth and share the facts as often as we can. This requires patient ministry.

Is this risky? You bet it is. Will we be used? Probably. But I believe that the Holy Spirit will protect His true Church.

Fifth, we must carefully increase publicity efforts — without jeopardizing Chinese leaders. The best way to turn back the darkness is to expose it to the light. It should be the business of the whole Christian world to mark criminals who violate human and civil rights. These atrocities against religious freedom must be exposed.

Human rights violations, martyrdoms, and vandalism need to be reported honestly and quickly. Since tyrants often have seared consciences, it is sometimes our duty to be their conscience and shame them into doing right. This prophetic role of the Church is often forgotten today — particularly in the West.

Letters to prisoners and visits to jails and labor camps often result in improved living conditions. Visits to churches and pilgrimages to the graves and sites of martyrdoms are also important. Memorializing the past will help save lives and freedoms in the future.

However, we must respect the advice and counsel of real Chinese Christian leaders in our publicity efforts. Great discernment is needed because propagandists use threats of retribution to prevent publicity as well.

It is best to avoid names and locations in publicity unless the local pastors and leaders involved are willing to reveal themselves. Publicity can result in beatings, jail and even death so they must be willing to expose themselves.

Sixth, support separation of church and state. Chinese rulers, scholars, and the Communist party have never accepted the notion of church/state separation. There is no historical Chinese model for "rendering unto Caesar that which is Caesar's, and rendering unto God that which is God's" as Christ taught us.

In fact, the TSPM appears at times and places to be trying to impose a kind of "Marxist Episcopacy" upon the local church, following the Anglican model of the British Isles. Just as state attempts to control the church in England resulted in some of the most shameful pages in British history, the same thing is being repeated in China today.

Chinese political scientists need to review the long history of failed "State churches" in Europe and the Middle East and study the teachings of Christ more closely. If they can try to better understand the true nature of kingdom of God, perhaps the Church will be less threatening to them. Perhaps also, they will soon enjoy more of the benefits that will come to China from religious freedom — such as the voluntary charity of a free church.

Seventh, call upon political leaders to fill their roles. The first purpose of government is to protect the lives and rights of it's citizens. In America, we can freely petition our government in public to enforce laws protecting freedom of religion and other basic human rights. This does not work in Chinese culture. Not only is public petitioning illegal, but it often brings retribution.

Christians need to use the freedoms we enjoy here in the States more often, calling upon our president to use his diplomatic influence in private negotiations with the Chinese. Then we need to support him and his staff with prayer and every other encouragement as they face the Chinese and seek religious freedom.

In addition, we can discreetly use every opportunity we have to privately write letters and meet with Chinese leaders, being led by the Holy Spirit.

The new Basic Law in Hong Kong will give Christians many new opportunities to dialogue with the Chinese government. The law guarantees many freedoms to the people of Hong Kong that are not allowed in China, including much greater freedom of religion and the continuation of a wide range of ministries and outreaches. Beijing has promised religious and media freedom to the British, to the people of Hong Kong, and to the international community in Hong Kong. This presents a great opportunity for the Chinese to "save face" by keeping their promises of religious freedom.

Eighth, don't give up. The dragon needs to know

that we won't quit. Terrorism and wars of attrition are antichrists favorite weapons — and he has gotten used to using them successfully against the Chinese. However, the dragon does change. He does transform himself. He does quit when we resist. That is the promise of God's Word. He does try "new tricks" when he finds that an old one is no longer working.

Just as the Emperor Constantine turned the Roman Empire from paganism to Christianity for political purposes, the dragon may find it in his best interests to allow religious freedom in China. Perhaps this freedom will only be temporary — but we must not let it take us by surprise.

I have hope for the 21st century. I have hope for religious freedom in China. Human history is not in the hands of the dragon, the United States, or the United Nations — and certainly not in any political party. Jesus Christ is the Lord of history. In the end, Romans 8:28 and 8:35-39 applies to the Church in China just as it applies in each of our personal struggles with the world, the flesh, and the devil.

For the suffering Church, the Bible promises that "we are more than conquerors through Him who loved us." Paul gives a long list of the trials that cannot separate us from God: tribulation, distress, persecution, famine, nakedness, peril, sword, death, life, angels, principalities, powers, things present and things to come, height, depth nor "any created thing."

The list sounds hauntingly familiar to any student of church history in China. The dragon is making a losing war on the church and will continue to make war on us. But he cannot separate us from Christ and His love — and he cannot defeat us unless we give up!

[1]Harry Wu, *Laogai: the Chinese Gulag* (New York, NY: Times Books, Random House, 1996), p. 309.

Chapter 7

The Dragon's War on the Church

> *On this rock I will build my church, and
> the gates of Hades shall not prevail against it
> . . . and whatever you bind on earth shall be
> bound in heaven* (Matt. 16:18-19).

When the Red Dragon saw the land of China — his greatest territory — falling to the kingdom of God, his first response was murderous. Then, in the 20th century, he added a relentless campaign of attrition and apostasy — seeking to politicize, control and weaken local churches through the Three Self Patriotic Movement. His final campaign against the Church, still to come, will seek to combine the churches in China with all other religious congregations of the world to form a giant super-church. To this "mega-church" the Antichrist will present his own image, the Beast, for worship.

The dragon's all-out war of violence on the Church of China reached it's zenith in the 19th and 20th centuries, and we are still living in that era. The Devil has put the world "on notice" about the Church in China. He threatens to charge any price "in human blood" to prevent the gospel from spreading in China. He relies on the weapons that have always worked for him before, terror and violence.

The Dragon and Stalinism

For this bloody task, Satan was able to enlist the ideal persecutor — a man and a party that already believed in terrorism; one that promised to brutally crush the infant Church with maximum force.

The communism of Joseph Stalin in the 1930s was the perfect weapon to provide such total opposition to the newly indigenous Chinese churches. Masterminded by Lenin and fine-tuned in the skills of extermination, its agents trained Mao Tse Tung's cadre in the grim arts of KGB-style police terror.

Communist hardliners in China are still without conscience. Cancerous. Double-minded. They can't seem to make up their mind about how to best destroy the Christian church. They infiltrate, take over, and ruthlessly exploit religion with one hand, even as they seek to destroy it with the other.

Using Religion of Political Ends

Christian denominations, congregations, hospitals, media, orphanages, schools, and religious institutions in China were allowed to survive ONLY as long as they helped serve "short-term" political purposes — and that turned out to be a very short-term indeed.

Ironically, Communist cadre could not see the historic link between Christian compassion, biblical morality, and the idealism of Karl Marx and Lenin! The early Communists were seeking nothing less than the imposition of Christian standards on secular society — without the transforming Lordship of Jesus Christ. It was a political Tower of Babel.

When Christian institutions proved unfruitful in whipping up patriotism for the Korean War, the Communists saw no value in keeping the facade up. Within nine years they managed to drive the local church underground and wipe out almost all visible traces of Christianity in China. They did this through a campaign of "decapitation" — cutting off the head of the snake — by eliminating bishops, pastors, and priests.

Working by the Numbers

Today, Communist persecution in China still "works by the numbers." They either use the Church as a propaganda tool — or seek to destroy it. But since communism can only deal with the materialistic and scientific world, it has been powerless to really affect the inner spiritual lives of the Chinese.

Communists leaders seem honestly puzzled by this inability to provide moral leadership. Current campaigns seek to develop a Communist morality or Chinese version of the "new socialist man" that the Soviets idealized in Russia.

Articles in the press and official directives from Beijing lament the fact that local cadres are attracted to Christianity — or seem reluctant to harass and "struggle against" their innocent, peaceful Christian neighbors! The truth is that many local Communist leaders are attracted to lifestyles of Christian citizens and the power of God that flows through their lives. Christians are outstanding, model citizens of new China — and peacefully co-exist with the Communist party when they are allowed to do so!

In fact, Christians practice the selfless, responsible love for their neighbors that communism seeks to impose by violence.

Fighting a Losing Battle

Yet the Communist hardliners, like Pharaoh in ancient Egypt, just don't seem to realize the power they are up against. You simply can't fight God and win. They will not be able to kill the Church. It doesn't matter how many campaigns they launch to "clean up the problem of religion."

It was relatively easy to steal Christian property, close down church buildings, and register one or two "TSPM show churches" in the fifties. This gave the appearance of religious freedom. These show churches were allowed to stay open as museums for propaganda purposes. However, no matter how many billions of dollars the Communists spend to destroy and infiltrate the Christian community, they still cannot contain the Holy Spirit. The life of God resides in the true body of Christ — not in holy buildings or Christian institutions. It is the invisible kingdom of God and materialistic attacks cannot destroy it. The ever-creative spark of divine life is alive and actively working in the hearts of Chinese believers!

Anti-Foreign Hatred and the Church

Inspiring Mao's terror campaign against the Church was nothing new for the dragon. Chinese criminal triads, emperors, and warlords have long-exploited Chinese fears and ignorance of foreigners. One reason the dragon has so enjoyed using China as his lair, has been this historic Chinese fear of outsiders. This nationalistic element was worked into all the Communist party inspired persecutions of the Church.

Dr. Jonathan Chao in his indispensable book on the Church in China, *Wise As Serpents, Harmless As Doves*, describes the Communist confrontation with the Church as merely an extension of latent feudalism.

He says:

The relation of church and state in socialist China basically follows the pattern of state control of religions in traditional China. The parallel between the two is very obvious:

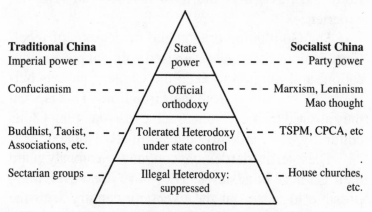

Traditional China		Socialist China
Imperial power – – – – – –	State power	– – – – – – – Party power
Confucianism – – – – – –	Official orthodoxy	– – – – Marxism, Leninism Mao thought
Buddhist, Taoist, – – – Associations, etc.	Tolerated Heterodoxy under state control	– – – TSPM, CPCA, etc
Sectarian groups – –	Illegal Heterodoxy: suppressed	– – House churches, etc.

In the matter of state control of religion, the present totalitarian socialist state inherited the position of the former feudalistic, imperial state. Hence, it may be said that current Chinese Communist religious policy is both totalitarian and feudalistic.[1]

So, the Communist persecution is really nothing new after all! They are actually only extending the centuries old policy of the dragon toward revealed truth. He wants to keep China in spiritual darkness! Just like all of China's historic political elites, communism has an unbroken history of hating the will of Almighty God — and portraying it as something "un-Chinese" or "foreign."

The Communists are actually using variations on centuries-old Chinese assimilation techniques to absorb, compromise, and co-opt the preaching of Christian truth. Just as the old empires used "education and examination" to produce conformity, the Communists use modern propaganda techniques and media manipulation. An individual, personal commitment to Christ as Lord and Saviour is the most hated of all religious experiences.

The God-hating dragon and his legions of rebellious demons have always abused political power, education, and religion to keep the Chinese nations hermetically sealed off from their true Lord. This is what they are still trying in vain to achieve — keeping China culturally, economically, and spiritually isolated.

These territorial demons continue to jealously guard their Chinese bondslaves. They have done everything possible to close out the twentieth century with the Chinese people still shrouded in spiritual darkness. The Communists were willing to kill at least 30 million innocent people in order to keep the light of the gospel out — and the slaughter still continues. Harry Wu believes there are between 90-100 million captives now in the "Laogai" labor camps where most of the first 30 million Chinese disappeared.

Compromise of Early Jewish Witness

The dragon's effort to isolate China began 1,000 years before Christ. Jewish merchant caravans traded widely throughout China, and the Jewish Diaspora even established communities among the Chinese. The law of God was visible in His covenant people who were preparing the way for Messiah to come. They had to be stopped.

First these Jews had to be spiritually compromised through the native folk idolatry of China. Then the dragon developed Confucianism and Taoism in the Han Dynasty (206 B.C.-A.D. 221). Finally, the Jews of China were physically eliminated through economic and marriage alliances with Chinese nobility. Eventually the light of Moses and the prophets was extinguished. The Jews of China were slain bloodlessly by the sword of racial assimilation.

Only a trained, spiritual-sensitive eye can find the bits of biblical truth that remain in the Chinese alphabet, culture, and royal traditions. But the light left was rarely enough to produce saving faith by itself. It would not be until the Christian era that the light of God's revelation would again shine in China.

Genocide of the Nestorians

No record of the early Christians exists in China. Apparently, lay believers among the first century Christian traders failed to witness to their neighbors or establish reproducing congregations. Perhaps the antichrist spirit resident in China was so sensitive to the danger that he snatched the seed away before the Word took root. At any rate, the first time we find historical records of established Chinese Christians isn't until

A.D. 635 when Nestorian Christians appeared in Northern China.

During the Tang Dynasty, the dragon allowed a brief window of spiritual openness to the rest of the world. Along with the Nestorians, Buddhist missionaries came from India. Migrations of Jews and many other religious teachers also came from Central Asia. Islam, Manichaeism, and Zoroastrianism appeared to prosper during this remarkable time of spiritual ferment.

Perhaps the dragon knew that he had to offer something new and stronger to counterattack the Nestorian Christians — so he allowed the powerful atheism of Buddhism to take root. The Buddhists brought with them an attachment to philosophy, self-improvement and spirit-worship. This combination of teachings quickly swept China and today many people in the West wrongly believe that it is a native, traditional Chinese religion!

After 210 years of light bearing, Nestorian Christians fell victims to mass-executions during the imperial persecution of Buddhist priests in 845. One account of the time tells of the massacre of 120,000 God-fearers — the Christians, Jews, and Muslims of a ninth century seaport. Scholars think it was probably modern-day Guangzhou. After that, the historical trail of Nestorian Christians seem to be lost for centuries.

Franciscan and Jesuit Persecutions

About 400 years later, Nestorian missionaries appear again as scribes and teachers in the courts of the Yuan dynasty (1279-1368). Under the Mongols, the Franciscan missionary John of Montecorvino also appears (1247-1328). His ministry to abandoned orphans failed to produce his dream — a native clergy for the tiny Catholic community he founded in the Yuan capital.

Jesuit giant Francis Xavier was the next missionary of record to come banging on China's door. However, the Ming Emperors forbid him to set foot on Chinese soil. He died on Shangchuan Island near Macao in 1552. His failure, however, focused for the first time the prayers of Christians. Around the world, Catholic believers began to storm the gates of "Old Cathay" in prayer. At last, the dragon's intransigence was recognized for what it is — a spiritual stronghold. At last, the need for spiritual warfare was seen by believers on every continent. In churches, convents, monasteries, and schools thousands began to pray for China's bamboo curtain to fall.

Spiritual Warfare Wins Results

God had used Xavier to break down spiritual strongholds in India, Siam, and many other lands — yet China remained a goliath, boasting of its self-sufficiency without the Lord who created it.

Jesuit missionary Matteo Ricci replaced Xavier. After 18 years of careful bridge-building, he was finally permitted to come to Beijing. Prayer and spiritual-warfare prevailed for the first time. In 1601, he was appointed a scientific consultant and advisor to the government. For the next 123 years, the Jesuits enjoyed a favored position in Qing dynasty courts through accommodation, compromise, education, and skillful political maneuvering. Their Machiavellian presence opened the doors to Dominican and Franciscan priests, who were able to establish the first viable Chinese Catholic congregations.

The Dragon's Revenge

However, in 1724 the dragon lashed back at the worldly activism of the Jesuits. He would not allow the Church to play "his game" and win. Papal interference in "ancestor worship" brought about the first power struggle between the Chinese emperor and the bishop of Rome. As a result all Catholic missionaries were expelled from the Grand Palace. Chinese believers were pressured to recant. Chinese native missionaries were executed by strangulation. This anti-Catholic persecution continued off and on until 1860. It is still carried on today — not only against the bishop of Rome but against all post-Constantine, Episcopal denominations. Their fatal mistake is daring to demand any outside allegiance to non-Chinese, foreign headquarters. Chinese nationalism can never be overestimated. No church movement that expects Chinese to report to non-Chinese, foreign headquarters has ever succeeded in China.

Through government, the Red Dragon has always insisted on controlling the religious and personal morality of the Chinese people. Just controlling the affairs of state has never been enough for him! This totalitarian policy is gleefully carried on today by the new "Communist Mandarins" of modern China.

However, God's Holy Spirit was at work in Catholic missions. When the Communists finally succeeded in forcing out the Catholic missionaries in 1949, they found that the "foreign devils" had left behind 2,698 ordained Chinese priests and 3.2 million baptized believers in Christ! Today, Catholics have developed several indigenous movements in the country that maintain local autonomy as well as an underground Catholic church loyal to Rome. Except for the Three Self Patriotic Catholic movement, most of the Catholics are still outside of the dragon's control.

Protestant Persecutions Begin

At the dawn of the 19th century however, God raised up an exciting new movement of the gospel which would successfully sweep across China. This spiritual revolution was transforming millions of individuals in the British Empire and her former American colonies. From this "Bible reading" revival, Protestant lay missionaries began fanning out around the globe. They soon started appearing in the treaty ports of China.

By developing personal piety, study of vernacular Bible translations, and obedience to Christ's Great Commission, these evangelical movements eventually established local churches in every corner of China.

It is this final move of the Holy Spirit that continues today wherever Chinese is spoken throughout the world. Despite intense Public Security Bureau persecution through arrests, beatings, jail, and sadism — native Chinese missionaries continue to multiply and carry forward the gospel left behind by these 19th century "apostles."

For the first 50 years, they were confined mostly to the port cities. However, after the western colonial powers forced open the doors to inland China trade in 1860, Christians in the West reacted with one of the greatest missionary crusades of all times.

To sense some of the incredible fervor of their push, listen to some of the typical rhetoric of John Angell James. This quote is from a passionate, 57-page pamphlet he wrote denouncing the opium trade and calling for missions to China:

China is open! — open from one end to the other for the introduction of the Gospel. I can imagine Morrison, Medhurst, and other departed missionaries rising from their seats in glory and uttering the shout, "China is open to the Gospel," while the heavenly host in millions echo the cry: "Hallelujah, China is open!"

Western Christians, does not God call to you from China to consider His ways? Could an audible voice from heaven be more intelligible? Do you not see Divine Providence beckoning you from Peking? Why comparatively few years ago it was death to a Chinese to embrace, and to a missionary to preach, the gospel. You ought — you must — you will do something more, much more for China. The fields are white unto harvest . . . I entreat Christians of all evangelical churches to rise in one might mass and exclaim, "China for Christ, China for Christ, God wills it!"

China's Inland Missions

Many missionaries like Hudson Taylor heard the same call in Shanghai and rushed into the new "open door." He loved the Chinese and Chinese culture and the Chinese knew it. Like so many other 19th century missionaries, his body lies buried with his wife and several children in the soil of China.

When Taylor saw the interior fling open, he began to appeal for 1,000 volunteers to adopt Chinese dress and customs — following him up the mighty Pearl and Yangtze rivers to preach Christ. Thousands of China lovers left middle-class homes in the West to join his China Inland Mission.

Soon their missionary graves began appearing in every corner of China. The work was hard and dangerous. From the start, numerous anti-missionary riots were inspired by jealous Mandarins and landlords. Local politicians resented the missionary clinics, schools, and zealous street preaching of the foreigners. The missionaries preached against opium addiction, foot binding, gambling, prostitution, and a host of social injustices.

They gained many enemies from among criminals, landlords, and exploiters of the people. Opposition from those in high places inspired racist hatred and fueled the ignorant prejudice of mobs against them. In the most famous of these anti-foreign riots, the "Boxers" killed over 200 missionaries and 2,000 Chinese believers in 1900.

Although there were periods of calm, this demon-inspired xenophobia continued to boil just beneath the surface. In 1926-27, between the World Wars, nearly all the 8,000 missionaries had to evacuate their inland stations. Anti-Christian and anti-foreign propagandists had learned how to effectively stir up hatred against the missionaries.

By 1949, when the 5,600 Protestant missionaries were finally forced to flee the people they loved, they had planted seeds that would grow to the end of time. They left thousands of primary and secondary schools to the people as well as 13 Christian universities. During the short 100 years they had been allowed in China, the missionaries also built thousands of hospitals, orphanages, and publishing houses. They introduced modern education, justice, health, and science along with the gospel of the Lord Jesus — laying the foundation for the modern China of today.

But the greatest legacy of the brief Protestant mission era were the 840,000 believers they left behind, meeting in 20,000 small congregations. Among these were 8,500 evangelists, 3,500 "Bible women" teachers, and 2,100 ordained pastors.

The Persecution of Chinese Believers

All anti-foreign persecution pales when one begins to measure the suffering of China's native churches and missionaries under the Communists.

The New Culture movement in the 1920s, and the steady drumbeat of anti-foreign propaganda by the Communists forewarned Chinese Christian leaders. It spurred their vision for building indigenous churches.

Long before the Communists started, the Holy Spirit was already leading the fathers of the Chinese church to develop an indigenous ecclesiology suited to their culture. Based on the primitive New Testament mode, rather that the western models of church polity, it would be strong enough to survive in the Orient.

The Chinese church that is growing today under Communist persecution could never be Catholic, Episcopal, independent, Presbyterian, or congregational in government. It would require an Asian structure like the New Testament churches of Antioch, Corinth, or Ephesus. Chinese leaders like Watchman Nee and Wang Mingdao knew this and planned accordingly.

But even then, it took 40 years of fire and bloodshed to purge and polish the Chinese bride of Christ into the vibrant churches seen in China today. It is one of the strongest and fastest-growing Christian movements in the world, and an excellent model for reforming the 21st century churches in Russia and the western democracies.

"Cell church" movements, copying the success of the Chinese model, are springing up throughout Asia and the West. They thrive, not only under dictators and totalitarian state churches, but wherever there is a need for evangelism, lay leadership, and rapid growth.

Stalin's Plan to Crush the Chinese Church

Since China did not have a state church — such as the Russian Orthodox and Ukrainian Orthodox sects in the former USSR — the Chinese Communists quickly discovered that Stalin's "top-down" church-wrecking strategies didn't work. They could not just control the Church by shooting priests, turning parish churches into factories, and infiltrating the hierarchy with KGB agents.

Classical international communism mistook the work of the Holy Spirit in Asia as mere "cultural imperialism" by the western powers. This was Lenin's big mistake in Asia. The Jeffersonian revolution in America had already effectively separated church and Christian missions from the state. There was no longer a direct connection! Therefore the Chinese found that their rapid expulsion of foreign business, military assistance, and even missionaries had little effect on Chinese Christianity. The Chinese were already following an indigenous, Asian church-planting method!

Neither did their nationalization of international Bible societies, hospitals, Christian media, and schools kill off the Church in China. Chinese local churches were not defined by their institutions. Clearly, another method was needed to infiltrate, control, minimize, and eventually destroy the Church. It was Chou En Lai who came up with a classical Communist strategy.

Chou En Lai's Plan to Create the TSPM

Working with a Communist leader who had infiltrated the YMCA movement, Wu Yaozong, Chou called a weekend retreat to brainstorm and come up with ideas. His plan was to recruit compromised, worldly or apostate Chinese Christian leaders to organize a Christian front organization for the churches. Communist cadres would thus be able to harness grass-roots Christian organizations to support Chinese involvement in the Korean War.

As a result of the meeting, the group formed a united front of church leaders to support Communist political plans. They borrowed the "three-self concept" from a missionary priest's classic book *Missionary Methods: St. Paul's or Ours?* It taught that Chinese churches should be self-supporting, self-governing, and self-propagating. The united front organization would be called The Three Self Patriotic movement (TSPM).

The plan involved writing a rather innocent-sounding "Christian Manifesto" which was to be signed by 40 denominational leaders who would, of course, been unable to sign the atheistic "Communist Manifesto." It called on all church leaders to support "New China" and break fellowship with Christians overseas.

The dragon was cleverly at work here by offering the presbytery a half-truth. He insisted that they pledge to separate themselves from the rest of the body of Christ by becoming "self-supporting, self-governing, and self-propagating." Since nearly all true Christian leaders in the local churches were already committed to the "three self" concept, it was hard not to sign.

However, those who saw through the ploy — and could not voluntarily sign with a clear conscience — set themselves up for an accusation campaign. To the Communists, they had proven themselves "unpatriotic" and "unfriendly" to the party and the state. By 1954 the Three Self Patriotic movement was fully organized and had built a national organization, funded and staffed by atheistic party officials. The TSPM is not, and has never been, a "state church" or denomination — although this idea has been widely circulated by propaganda in the West.

Pressure began to mount on individuals who had still not signed. Finally all local congregations were required to register and sign or be branded as "counter-revolutionary." After TSPM registration, pastors found themselves fully under control of the local Communist party apparatus. The trap was so successfully designed that similar "Three Self" fronts were organized to politicize Buddhists and Catholics in 1957.

By 1957, unregistered pastors and congregations were nearly all identified and easily closed down on various pretexts. Then the pastors who had signed their loyalty to communism were purged next. They were required to leave their flocks for "six months" to do "political studies" at re-education camps. Meanwhile, the sheep were scattered. Most pastors never returned after they discovered they were part of the "exploiter class" and should return to farm and factory work.

The TSPM was so effective in suppressing local church congregations that by the end of 1958 only eight of the 200-plus churches in Shanghai were left. In Beijing, the 66 Protestant congregations were reduced to 4! The same story was being repeated all over China.

The Agony Begins in Earnest

In *The China Mission Handbook,* Jonathan Chao and scholars from Chinese Church Research Center in Hong Kong have tracked what happened next into seven periods of oppression:

(1) THE CHURCH SUPPRESSED (1958-66) — Heavy-handed control of the TSPM congregations by the Religious Affairs Bureau meant an end to Christian education and Sunday schools, evangelism, and community outreach. Without their pastors, what was left of the other congregations began to meet clandestinely in homes. When caught, they were rounded up and thrown into slave labor camps. Many disappeared for 10-20 years or are still missing. Yet in the camps, the gospel spread among prisoners — and believers learned how to go underground. The house church movement was thus implemented out of necessity where it had not already been implemented by design.

(2) THE CHURCH IN SUFFERING (1966-76) — The Great Cultural Revolution was Mao's ultimate attempt to destroy Christ's body in China. When Mao and his "Gang of Four" unleashed frenzied mobs of Chinese baby-boomers on the Church, Christians began their worst period of suffering. All law and order broke down as millions of teenagers looted the homes of Christians looking for "old ideologies, old customs, old morals, and old habits." Even the apostate leaders of TSPM were "struggled against" and their "seminary" in Nanjing became the Red Guard headquarters.

Red Guards were so blinded with hatred of Christ that even atheistic Communist party members among the TSPM clergy were added to the list of martyrs for Christ! The Communists were turning on themselves in confusion and killing their own infiltrators.

The few Bibles and hymnbooks left were burned. Christians were dragged through the streets to be humiliated and beaten. Many died or were left injured — some paralyzed for life. All Christian meetings, both legal TSPM groups and house fellowships, were ended. However in 1969, as Christians around the world prayed for China, supernatural events were reported from all the provinces of China. The living God was coming to the aid of His people.

Young men were being led by the Holy Spirit to meet in small groups of 5-10 to recite the New Testament Book of Peter and other Scriptures from memory. They encouraged one another to "suffer for his sake" (Phil. 1:29). Even as all semblance of civilization crumbled around them, these leaderless "suffering groups" grew. Many had 50-200 members by the end of the Cultural Revolution. Miraculous healings, supernatural signs, and wonders confounded those who attended — and the Church began growing again with millions of new converts who were willing to "take up their cross of suffering" and follow the Lord Jesus.

(3) THE RISEN CHURCH (1976-80) — With the death of Mao and demise of the "Gang of Four" and Hua Guofeng, China's new strong man Deng Xiaoping needed to restore order. The Communist party apparatus was reformed and with it the TSPM was resurrected and reorganized. For a time, the persecution of "house churches" became a back-burner item. A brief window of freedom flung open in 1979-80. Miraculous healings, deliverances, and conversions continued. Many Communist cadres even accepted Christ and semi-public meetings became commonplace.

(4) THE CHURCH IN SPIRITUAL CONFLICT (1980-82) — By now, the Christian community in China had reached about 50 million members, over 50 times larger than when the Communists took control. Itinerant Chinese missionaries were crisscrossing the country to preach discreetly. The reorganized TSPM was growing increasingly jealous of the growing house churches.

The Central Committee of the Communist Party issued Document No. 19 in March of 1982. It outlined "Three Designates" to clamp down again on Christian worship, stop itinerant evangelism, and close house churches. It mandated that Christians could only worship in TSPM buildings, only TSPM pastors could preach, and TSPM pastors could only preach in their own districts. Waves of arrests and new persecution followed.

(5) THE CHURCH UNDER PERSECUTION (1983-84) — Using the "Three Designates" as an excuse, the TSPM began working closely with secret police to track down traveling evangelists. Using planted infiltrators to accuse lay believers, they were able to close more house fellowships. The Religious Affairs Bureau coordinated a nation-wide crackdown on Christian citizens which included much physical punishment, torture, and long prison terms — sometimes using threats of torture simply to get believers to renounce their faith in Christ. Sadistic PSB police routinely use beatings, electric shock, water torture, sleep deprivation, rape, and sexual abuse to "question" Christians about their belief.

While most house churches were simply forced further underground during this campaign, about 1,200 house churches did register with the TSPM — which seems to have been the reason for the increased persecutions. However, the harshness of the campaign once again backfired on the Communists. The attacks seemed to let up some in the last half of the decade.

(6) THE MISSIONARY CHURCH (1985-89) — Although TSPM and police persecution of house groups continued in 1984, the Central Committee significantly shifted focus. Deng's economic goals were focusing the Party away from ideological struggle to economic reform. The dragon seemed to once again have temporarily lost interest in destroying the Church. A rash of legal advances occurred, and it seemed like the Christians were being accepted again as an institution. The Amity Press was opened to print Bibles and literature on the mainland for the first time since the revolution. Some foreign development aid was accepted. Even foreign Christian tentmakers were being allowed in to teach English. Both the house churches and the TSPM were organizing programs to train clergy — TSPM in ten legal seminaries and the house churches in 11 short-term "Seminaries in the Field." The dragon let Christians begin to relax again, feeling that some kind of accommodation with his agents was becoming reality. Quietly and modestly, both the TSPM and the house groups began planning for the future. Hope began rising. Chinese native missionaries were sent to frontier areas. But then came the collapse of communism in the USSR and Eastern Europe, the democracy movement, and the Tiananmen Square massacre.

(7) THE CHURCH FOLLOWING TIANANMEN SQUARE (1989-present) — The overnight collapse of communism in the USSR, Hungary, Poland, and

Czechoslovakia was closely monitored by the worried Chinese Central Committee. Documents about the surprisingly active role of Christians and Catholic Christians in democracy movements were widely distributed throughout the Party. Many Chinese hardliners believed that Christian revivals in Eastern Europe were a major reason for the collapse of communism — sometimes even precipitating the fall of European dictators.[2]

What's more, Polish Pope John Paul II of Wadowice (the first Catholic pontiff raised under Marxism) was extraordinarily skillful in circumventing Communist restrictions. It was obvious that he was very actively using the new freedoms in China to re-establish close ties with "faithful" Roman Catholics. (This has resulted in a very brutal and determined new persecution of Catholics, including police abductions of clergy, much extra-judicial detention of priests and bishops, torture and deaths of at least three bishops while in police custody.)

Christian demonstrators were also reported among the students massacred in Tiananmen Square — mostly from Communist-controlled TSPM congregations in Beijing and Nanjing! Bishop Teng, one of the old guard Communist leaders of the TSPM, was widely quoted as favoring the student demonstrations in the early days of Tiananmen.

The challenge of controlling the strong, free Cantonese Christian congregations in Hong Kong also presents an interesting new problem to the Religious Affairs Bureau in Beijing . . . one that will be closely watched for the next few years.

These many movements, all coming together at the same time, have fueled the fears of Communists about the ever-growing Christian community. Church membership is much larger than the Communist Party. Christians, while inactive politically, are seen by power-hungry young Communists as a potential threat.

This is resulting in new campaigns of persecution in every part of China, and an increase in their wary surveillance of the Christian churches.

Some of the harassment of Christians appears to be simply from corrupt "rogue cops" who break up Christian house meetings, beat leaders, "confiscate" personal belongings as "evidence," and collect unreasonable "fines" on the spot. All this corruption is done without judicial hearings, independent legal counsel for the accused, or concern for the civil or human rights of innocent believers.

But the persecution goes much deeper than that. Beijing could stop such abuses in a day if it cared. It is tightening up the party and police apparatus nationwide in preparation for 2000 and beyond. Referred to officially as "zhonghe zhili" or "comprehensive rule," the policy calls for consolidating control to better manage what Communists call "evil elements in society." Listed among them are various vices including prostitution and pornography, and some very Christian activities such as unregistered printing presses, holding religious meetings, and having more than one child.

How many countries in the world would officially describe operating a printing press, having a baby, or worshiping God as "evil activities?"

The Propaganda War in the West

No chapter on the dragon's war on the Chinese church could be complete without mentioning the collaboration of the councilor movement with the Communists. They have abetted the persecution of Chinese believers in two ways: with finances and propaganda cover.

Since 1985, cash-hungry Communists in the TSPM have found ways to start accepting foreign aid from western state churches and para-church organizations. While this is contrary to the "three self" manifesto they signed, hard currency is irresistible in modern China. No bureau of the government can survive without it — especially one that has to have budgets to buy modern computer communications and electronic spy technology in U.S. dollars.

To do so, they have permitted the development of a new series of front organizations such as the China Christian Council (CCC) and the Amity Press. These quasi-government organizations have provided the Communists with a great deal of credibility and even professional public relations in western nations.

The Council is especially important in getting international recognition for the TSPM. Although the TSPM is not actually a church by any definition, it is the only group permitted to "dialogue" with western Christians, church leaders, denominations, journalists, theologians, tourists, and scholars.

Through dis-information campaigns, propaganda, and controlled media events the TSPM and CCC have been able to effectively use western third parties as spokespersons. They portray to the outside world a deceptive picture of China's state-controlled churches — congregations that are free to worship and evangelize, that are developing and growing, and which have united to overcome old denominational barriers.

As a result, some western Christian leaders unwittingly become tools of the dragon — failing to identify themselves with Christ's suffering Church in China. In fact, some have joined in with the Communists, blaming the "underground church" for their own persecution!

Pastor Dennis Balcombe of Revival Christian Church, Hong Kong, eloquently speaks for the Chinese victims, expressing the outrage of their situation:

> To claim that persecution is made greater than necessary by the provocation of Chinese Christians makes the victim of injustice the criminal and only justifies the illegal and often criminal activities of God-hating men who use the lack of freedoms guaranteed by the Chinese Constitution to imprison, fine, and beat up law-abiding Christians.

> It is equivalent to stating a woman deserved to be raped because she is a woman or a wealthy man deserved to be robbed because he is wealthy. Nobody has heard of Christians taking a political stand, demonstrating against the government, demanding anything or doing anything that would provoke officials. They only want to be left alone to serve God, go to church, train their young people and future leaders, and preach the Gospel.

> It must be clearly stated that the Christians have done nothing nor said anything to justify the horrendous persecution that they have had to endure. They are hard-working honest people who should be the pride of their nation.

... during the past 45 years of the control of the Communist party of China, the majority of Christians outside China have stood on the side of those persecuting the Church and have continually criticized the victims of this injustice. It has been especially true of western church leaders. I would hope that they are simply ignorant of the situation in China and have not chosen deliberately to take a stand against the members of their Body. As Paul said, "And whether one member suffer, all the members suffer with it" (1 Cor. 12:26).

The Victorious Chinese Church

The whole Christian world needs to be praying daily for the Chinese and support them as they go through these bloody birthpangs. Our own spiritual futures are intimately linked to the Chinese in many ways.

First, Christ will not return for us until His Chinese body is completely formed. "And this Gospel of the Kingdom shall be preached in all the whole world for a witness unto all nations; and then shall the end come," says Christ in Matthew 24:14. That means that every still-darkened corner of China needs to receive the gospel. Over one-fifth of the world's population lives in China and there is a great deal of evangelism still to be done. While there are some opportunities for outsiders to witness in China, only the Chinese can reach China for Christ.

Second, only Chinese can reach much of Central Asia. Tibet, Mongolia, and many parts of the middle-east and former USSR will be reached by Chinese missionaries in days to come. The Chinese have been tempered in the fires of suffering and are ready to pay the price to take the gospel into the Muslim world and other hostile environments.

Third, the quality of the Chinese Christian spirituality offers inspiration and renewal to the backslidden churches of the West. In China, the Church has not just formed a fresh polity. It also offers us a refreshing new model of piety that we desperately need.

The Church in China, says Pastor Balcombe, has much to teach the Western churches about: (1) Putting the emphasis on people rather than buildings; (2) Restoring the ministry to the laity rather than relying on a professional clergy class; (3) Learning ministry through discipleship rather than academic degrees; (4) Developing personal piety and empowerment by God rather than through entertainment, human talents, and platform ministries.

With the spiritual decline of the West, who knows if it will be America's turn to suffer persecution next? Chinese Communist persecutions have only proven to make the true Church stronger and bigger in China. Perhaps the same would happen to the USA after judgment comes to the house of God in North America.

Tony Lambert, research director for the China Ministries Department of OMF, says that despite the Communist persecution, the Church in China is well on the way to becoming the largest group of committed evangelical Christians in the World.

Many believe it has already happened, but Lambert estimates there are still only 33.6 million evangelical believers in China — 15 million less than the 49 million who claim to be "born again" in the United States. But insiders who know both worlds say that the Chinese already make up in zeal what they lack in numbers.

Others believe that China has already passed the USA both in numbers of believers and Spiritual strength.

At any rate, the dragon's war on the Church has been a disaster for Satan. Despite all the evidence of failure, the dragon's Beijing bureaucracy will not give up its plan to create a state-controlled, counterfeit church. Nor will it give up the plan to destroy or compromise the true body of Christ in China. This fact alone explains the diabolical intransigence with which the dragon deals with American and other Western Christians.

There is one piece missing in all this. The dragon knows that it isn't enough to just destroy the Church in China — he has to destroy the source of the Church. That means destroying the Word of God, especially the written Word of God.

[1]Jonathan Chao, *Wise as Serpents, Harmless as Doves: Christians in China Tell Their Story* (William Carey Library, 1988).

[2]Jonathan Chao, *The China Mission Handbook: a Portrait of China and Its Church* (Hong Kong: Chinese Church Research Center, 1989).

Chapter 8

The Dragon's War on the Chinese Bible

So shall My word be that goes forth from my mouth; It shall not return to Me void, but it shall accomplish what I please, And it shall prosper in the thing for which I sent it (Isa. 55:11;NKJV).

Nothing so terrifies China's tyrants — or the dragon spirit which controls them — as the Word of God. They fear the Bible in Chinese more than all other books or writings combined. Bibles are still being sought out and destroyed as if they were guns or bombs! And no wonder — since the Bible came to China there has been more social change in two centuries than the 30 that preceded them!

"Ye shall know the truth," promised Christ, "and the truth shall make you free" (John 8:32;NKJV). Since following His Word is what makes us His disciples (John 8:31) it is really the Bible that gives birth to the Church. The dragon knows this. To effectively kill the Christians and destroy the Church of China, he must stop the Bible.

For 3,000 years the dragon successfully struggled to guarantee that the light of God's Word did not shine in China. That gospel light finally punched through the spiritual darkness in the 19th century. That's when the first Chinese Bible appeared. It was the most revolutionary event in the history of the Middle Kingdom. China is still reeling from the impact of that first Bible translation — it broke the dragon's hold on his Chinese slaves for the first time ever!

The Bible proclaims liberty to the captives and thus helps fulfill the mission of Christ to this world — bringing healing and salvation to all the people of China.

China's Most Important Need

So the single most important thing any American can do to help the Chinese people today is to sponsor more Bibles for China. This is China's greatest need — more than child care, economic development, human rights, food, or even spiritual ministries like church planting. If the Bible gets in, all the other blessings of the Bible will follow as well.

That's why Bible distribution is still our number one ministry to China. Since we began, Nora Lam Chinese Ministries has been able to send over one million Bibles into China from Hong Kong. Right now, we're working on several "Bible Breakthrough" plans to provide millions of additional Bibles to China.

Thank God for the thousands of Americans who are still hand-carrying Bibles into China and helping us sponsor new printings of the Chinese Bible. Although sometimes it seems like only a trickle of Bibles are getting through, those Bibles are doing the work of an army of missionaries.

The Book He Kills to Stop

The dragon so fears the gospel in Chinese he still literally kills to keep it from reaching his remaining Chinese slaves. Thousands have died just for possessing a copy of the Bible in the last few years. A whole generation of Chinese Christian leaders was murdered to stop its message — and the persecution is still going on as I write.

For nearly five decades now, the dragon's Communist cadre has desperately tried to cut off all Bible supplies — and destroy the few copies already in the country. During the Cultural Revolution, millions of teenagers were instructed to go house-to-house collecting and burning Chinese Bibles. Millions of book burnings resulted. Hundreds of thousands died and went to slave labor camps during the Great Cultural Revolution. The emotional scars of this period are felt by every Chinese person who lived through that horror. Many Chinese still get shivers when they talk about those days which disgraced Mao and China in the eyes of the whole world. All that was for one purpose — to wipe out "old religious ideas" like the Bible!

Although they were dying, Mao and his cohorts felt the pain of the Cultural Revolution was worth it. From the standpoint of the Communist hardliners, it was all done for a very good reason. It was their last chance to rid China of the Bible and plunge the country back into ignorance and slavery. As far as I can tell, many of these hardliners would still repeat the disaster of the Cultural Revolution today — the dragon is still at heart a crazed, ruthless fanatic.

The dragon knows his doom is certain when the Chinese people have the Bible. The Bible tells the whole plan of God for their personal freedom, and the final failure of Antichrist's schemes for China. It also reveals God's blueprint for salvation, church life, and morality based on the obedience and righteousness that comes voluntarily through faith. This is a different kind of morality than the collective conscience the dragon has created for China. His brand of Chinese morality is based on fear, pain, pleasure, punishment, and shame.

Each Bible Wins Five to Christ

The dragon fears the Bible because this book alone has the power to generate a new world view among its Chinese readers.

"Often God's written Word is the only tool available — or needed — for people to find Jesus Christ," says Lars Dunberg of the International Bible Society. IBS supplies one of the most popular Chinese study Bibles to the 600,000 Christians in Hong Kong. For years, many of these Bibles have steadily found their way across the border into China — often one at a time, hidden in the luggage of returning visitors.

Dedicated foreign tourists and business people also carry thousands of Bibles across the boarders of Hong Kong, still only a trickle of what is needed.

When caught receiving these Bibles, local pastors in China are regularly tortured and jailed. Their crime?

Possessing a Bible from Hong Kong. Yet the demand for these study Bibles increases all the time. Every Chinese pastor and leader wants a study Bible.

According to leaders of the China Harvest Bible-coalition, each Bible brought into China results in at least five Chinese finding Christ! China Harvest is one of the leading agencies coordinating joint printing and distribution of Bibles to China. Satan realizes that the Bible has the power to save souls — that the Lord has vowed to bless it — and so he works continually to block it. Every Bible which the dragon stops at the China border means five more Chinese souls will suffer in the flames of hell for all eternity.

Millions Spent to Stop Bible Imports

The dragon knows the Bible is far more dangerous to his control of China than ideologies like Marxism or Jeffersonian democracy. No surprise. Hebrews 4:12 says, "The word of God is quick and powerful and sharper than any two-edged sword, piercing even to the division of soul and spirit, and of joints and marrow, and is a discerner of the thoughts and intents of the heart."

The Communist hardliners still struggle in vain to contain the force of this rare book — even as they ridicule it. Why? If the Bible is just myths and fables as their atheistic pamphlets claim, why are they so afraid of it? Communist professors in universities brainwash students against the Bible, but they won't let the students have a personal copy to read. In fact, it is kept under lock and key in university libraries! That doesn't sound like a book of fables to me — and Chinese students are not fooled either.

The Communist party and state agencies spend

millions of dollars annually to stop the free flow of Bibles. Plainclothes police ride the trains, looking for Bible couriers. Chinese are forced to smuggle the Bible from place to place like common criminals.

Banned Bibles Not for Sale

No matter how much money you have, you cannot buy the Bible in regular Chinese bookstores! In China you need a license both to print books and distribute them. No licenses to distribute Bibles are available — even though a very small amount of legal Bible printing is now allowed.

The Bible is never displayed, even when booksellers have copies on hand. When book dealers are able to find stocks of black-market Bibles to sell, they must hide them in the basement or under the counter. It is far easier to get pornography than a Bible in China. It is the single most dangerous book to own in China today. A Communist caught reading the Bible will soon be expelled from the Party. It ruins his future career both professionally and in the party.

Bibles in the Churches

Bibles are so rare that whole house congregations frequently share one edition. House church pastors travel days to pick up a personal copy in Canton, Shanghai, or other big cities where Bibles are available on the black market. Often, a new copy of the Scriptures is reverently cut apart into sections or pages. These are more easily circulated among the believers and harder for the secret police to confiscate. As a result, Scripture memorization is much more common in China than the West. Many believers can quote whole chapters and books by heart. In this way, even in "Laogai" slave labor camps and prisons, the Word of God is not stopped.

The modern battle for the Chinese Bible is such a big and exciting drama that we are writing a separate book just on this subject. Anecdotal reports do escape government censors — even though Chinese risk jail to tell stories of their persecution — and I am collecting them for another book that will tell the whole exciting story of the battle for the Chinese Bible.

Historical Resistance to the Bible

Tyrants everywhere are afraid of the Bible in the language of the people. The Chinese aren't the only ones to oppose the Scripture! Even the British aristocracy resisted the publication of the Bible in English for 1,500 years. It wasn't until Wycliffe and Tyndale died to translate and publish it that it was finally available to the English people in their own language!

Robert Morrison was well aware of this when he came to China to translate the Bible. Speaking of bitter British and Chinese imperial opposition to work on his first Chinese Bible, he said the only thing that kept him from despair was remembering how the British kings had opposed the Bible in English — how they had wanted to keep it in Latin so only scholars and clergy could read and control it.

"I remember Britain," he wrote from China, "what she was, and what she now is in respect to (freedom of) religion. Three hundred years have not elapsed since national authority said that the Bible should not be read openly in any church by the people, nor privately by the poor; that only noblemen and gentlemen, and noble ladies and gentlewomen, might have the Bible in their homes. I remember this, and cherish hope for China."

The Dragon's Conspiracy Against the Bible

Although paper and printing were invented by the Chinese, both church and government officials stonewalled Chinese Bible translation and publishing for centuries. It was not until 1799 and 1807 that Joshua Marshman and Robert Morrison separately began their translation efforts.

The Red Dragon had successfully kept the Chinese Bible away from the people for 1,800 years. It was a mammoth, international conspiracy that required the help of Chinese emperors and mandarins, international kings and merchants in Europe or the Middle East, popes and clergy, as well as legions of intellectuals, literary and scholars.

Although historical records show that the Jewish colony of Kaifeng, China safely kept and studied their Torah scrolls in Hebrew for over 1,000 years — they were apparently never translated into Chinese! None of the Nestorian missionary literature survives either. Early Catholic missionaries, encouraged by Papal policy, rarely emphasized Scripture translation or publication. When they did, it was not in Chinese.

By the time Morrison arrived in China, British East India Company propagandists still insisted that by the nature of the language, it was impossible to translate Chinese into English! British opposition to his work was so strong, in fact, that he had to seek sanctuary in the American trade mission to China. The first translation work began under the stars and stripes.

However, nothing compared to the opposition he experienced from the Chinese mandarins. They forbid any Chinese native to teach the language to Morrison under penalty of death. The brave Cantonese scholar who finally agreed to help him carried poison at all times, ready to commit suicide rather than face a lingering death by torture.

At 25 years of age, Morrison had to compile dictionaries, lexicons, and study aids — before beginning the translation work from English, Greek, Hebrew, and Latin! Virtually a prisoner of Chinese authorities, he rented space in factory buildings and was not even permitted to go out for exercise.

Everything possible was done to keep the Chinese language a mystery and harass the work. His helpers were hunted down, imprisoned, and beaten. The men who cut his Chinese printing blocks where arrested and executed. Not permitted to openly translate, he secretly took "tentmaking work" as a clerk for the British East India Company, the powerful international trading monopoly that had resisted his coming in the first place!

This finally allowed him to develop Chinese/English translation tools for commercial purposes — and this in turn helped lead to the completion of the first Chinese Bible in 1823. Meanwhile, Marshman had been working separately on his translation in India. Both versions were completed the same year!

Free Distribution at Last!

By 1825, the first editions of the Chinese Bible were slowly being distributed by Bible societies around the world. This began a short-lived publishing and distribution enterprise in China that lasted for 124 years! But even though that breath of freedom was so short, the Word of God was planted deep in the soil of Chinese hearts.

With often bloody opposition, Chinese Bible Society "colporteurs" criss-crossed China, selling Bibles from village to village. As a result of that Bible distribution, there are probably well over 70 million Chinese believers on the mainland today.

Thousands of testimonies tell of villagers who converted to Christ after reading the "Glad Tidings" versions of John or Matthew. These pamphlets contained only one of the Gospels without commentary or notes. They sold for pennies and even the poorest peasant could afford to buy them. Millions were bought. Many stories are told of Chinese congregations beginning without missionaries — simply from reading the words of Jesus!

What the Dragon Hates Most in the Bible

All this was too much for the dragon. So, from the first days of secular humanists nationalism in China, he used the teachings of Marx and Lenin to "discredit" the message of the Bible. Eventually, propagandists even developed their own deadly alternative to the Bible — Mao's infamous little red book. *The Sayings of Chairman Mao* actually imitates the appearance of a pocket New Testament, and is used much the same way. His proverbs and sayings are studied by devout Communist youth, much as Christians study the Bible. Millions of copies of Mao's thoughts were distributed in order to replace the Bible during the Great Cultural Revolution.

Now, only two decades later, you can hardly find a copy of the little red book anywhere in China — even in the temples where worshipful Communists sit before idols of Mao "to absorb his spirit." Yet the demand for the Bible and the message of the Bible is constantly increasing — and the "New Communist" leaders are spending more time than ever trying to discredit the Bible.

Forbidden Bible Themes

In seeking to displace the Bible, hardline materialists have even forbidden TSPM pastors to preach on many biblical themes. They have even issued directives forbidding readings from certain books of the Bible such as Revelation and Daniel.

They point out four "superstitious messages" in the Bible which all Communists must struggle against. The Bible doctrines they most hate and fear are:

** CREATION — The Genesis message that "in the beginning God created" China is deeply anti-Marxist. Chinese Communists believe in atheistic evolution as the only explanation for existence. Their ideology is still married to 19th century evolution. Darwin's theory is still treated with religious reverence in Chinese universities. Man is simply an animal, taught Marx — nothing more that an accidental mix of matter and energy. Recognizing the spiritual side of man is politically incorrect at any level in modern China.

** ETERNITY — The Bible teaches that there is life after death, and judgment to come. Chinese materialism teaches that the present material world is all there is. For the leaders in Beijing, there must be no judgment seat of God. No heaven. No hell. No right. No wrong. For if they admit to these things, they can no longer justify the cannibalism, murder, and terror by which they rule. If there is life after death, they cannot justify their present lifestyles — an existence lived merely to satisfy the animal needs of their bodies: food, health, sex and shelter. The New Communists hardliners still believe that the Chinese can and should live "by bread alone."

They face a growing materialism and hedonism in today's godless Chinese culture that is a direct result of these "politically correct" ideologies of the 20th century. Just as these philosophies have destroyed whole generations of young people in the West, the Chinese are now discovering that they have drug problems, AIDS, and a host of culture-destroying social problems which they ironically blame on "western culture" — while all the time fighting the only book that can stop their culture decay.

** THE SECOND COMING — That Christ is returning soon to rule China as King of kings and Lord of lords is an unspeakable fact. This cuts against the core of what motivates the dragon-worshipping materialists in their quest for total power and control. Any teaching on the soon return of Christ is forbidden. Only the dragon can rule China through his modern-day mandarins. They cannot allow Jesus to be Lord of the Chinese, or any other people group living within the borders of the Chinese empire.

** DELIVERANCE, HEALING, AND MIRACLES — It is amazing to talk with underground house church pastors about the miracles they have experienced in the villages. One of the uncanny things you notice almost immediately is how their accounts sound almost exactly like stories from the Bible! God's Word is a book of miracles. The Bible takes it for granted that God will intervene in the material world. Jesus raises the dead, heals the sick, and casts out demons. Simple Chinese believers who read these stories, and start to believe in the Bible, begin to do these things. They see these miracles occur, even without hearing teachings about what can or cannot still happen today. The Jesus Christ of the Chinese church is the same yesterday, today, and forever.

This enrages the hardliners. In 1996, fresh orders from Beijing to TSPM congregations have repeated stern warnings against praying for healing. This is strictly forbidden and considered the worst kind of superstition. Pastors are told not to lead prayers for healing, lay hands on the sick, or take authority over demons that cause mental illness. Yet the reports keep coming of demons being cast out, diseases healed and even resurrections from the dead. These come from every province of China and seem to be part of the general spiritual revival in China today. The idea that Jesus Christ is alive and active today is very frightening to the dragon and his followers — the notion that God answers prayer must be stamped out at all costs.

So the dragon's battle against the Chinese Bible is fought at many levels. He seeks to destroy God's Word every chance he gets, and when he can't do that — he still wants to practice theology. One hardly thinks of the dragon as a Bible scholar or teacher, but he is tenacious and determined to undermine God's message to the Chinese. If he can't ban the Bible entirely, he does his best to make sure that "the whole counsel of God" is not getting through.

China Bible Distribution Today

Bible distribution in China today is at a major crossroads. Since 1949, Hong Kong has been the main source of Chinese Bibles — sometimes the only source.

At first, commercial presses printed beautiful, high-quality copies of the Holy Scriptures for the United Bible Societies there. Other Christian groups like the Gideons and New Life Literature Ltd. in Kowloon have also printed tons of Bibles in free Hong Kong.

However, inflation is making it cheaper to print Chinese Bibles in other places including Illinois, Indonesia, Malaysia/Singapore, Thailand, Vietnam, and even inside China itself.

So for economic reasons, Hong Kong's role in supplying Bibles for China is changing — especially if Beijing's restrictions on Bible publishing in China are extended to Hong Kong in the days ahead. However, the government in Beijing has promised that freedom of press and religion will continue in Hong Kong.

Even so, that does not mean that Hong Kong will continue to be the main source of supply for Bibles and other Christian products to China. The Basic Law under which Hong Kong is to be governed restricts the Church in Hong Kong from having ministry throughout the rest of China. The borders are likely to remain tightly sealed against Chinese Christian literature and products — either produced in Hong Kong or shipped through Hong Kong.

The future of Hong Kong's Christian publishing trade with the rest of China — both legal and illegal — will probably not be settled in the courts and legislatures. Again, spiritual warfare against the dragon combined with hard-headed business deals are going to be necessary.

If overseas Chinese Christians are serious about distributing Christian literature throughout China, they are going to have to deal with China's new Communist leaders in marketing terms. This will take the same kind of patience and relationship-building that any kind of other business with the Chinese takes.

We need to pray that God will raise up some Christian publishers who see this kind of business career as a calling. I believe that God's business in China should be done with at least as much integrity and professionalism as those who are selling Coca Cola and Wendy's hamburgers in China.

Bible Publication in China

Very limited publication and distribution of the Bible is permitted in China today. This highly-restricted Christian publishing industry is carried on in four ways:

(1) AMITY PRESS, NANJING — The most visible Bible publication in China is carried on by the Amity Press, a gift to China from the United Bible Societies (UBS). It was set up originally to print Bibles and other literature for congregations registered with the Three Self Patriotic movement.

Distribution of Amity Bibles however, remains extremely weak. Even when a Bible is published, that doesn't mean it will get into the hands of those who need and want it the most.

Every Chinese house church leader interviewed for this book complained that Amity Bibles rarely trickle down to the grass roots. This may be simply because the demand is so much greater than Amity can meet — but it also has a lot to do with man-made bottlenecks all along the distribution route. There are at least 35 million believers on the unofficial "waiting lists" for a personal Bible — and some leaders insist the market for Bibles in China right now is 2-3 times greater than that! It is amazing that the normally industrious Chinese cannot respond to this need in the primary market for Bibles.

In addition to the weak marketing system, local believers admit they are afraid to expose themselves by applying to TSPM congregations and distribution points for an officially printed Amity Bible.

(2) EAST GATE MINISTRIES — However in 1992, Ned Graham of East Gate Ministries International began making a series of financial grants to Amity Press for printing "house church" Bibles as well. His strategic agreement with Amity was signed by the China Christian Council (CCC) and the UBS as well. Though none of the house churches are members of the CCC, his Bibles are distributed exclusively to unregistered house churches. The East Gate contract is based on the unheard of idea that foreign aid is allowed to come "openly and transparently" through government-controlled agencies to the unregistered local churches.

Ned Graham sums it up well. "Relationships are our most important resource in China, and the fundamental basis for any relationship is trust. We do everything we can to build and maintain relationships established on trust with the government, the Three Self Patriotic movement, the CCC and within the house church community." Unfortunately for Rev. Graham, that trust is seldom reciprocated. Too many have died, been tortured, and disappeared for the Bible in order for Chinese believers to trust the government supply lines for Bibles.

Unfortunately, East Gate has only been able to distribute about 1.2 million Bibles so far — less than .02 percent of what the house churches need, if you accept that there are 50 million believers in the underground churches.

(3) RELIGIOUS AFFAIRS BUREAU — A third publisher of Bibles and religious literature is the Religious Affairs Bureau in Beijing — the government watchdog organization set up to suppress and supervise religion in China! Cash-starved, the RAB is also willing to receive outside funds in U.S. dollars in order to expedite Bible publishing, and the production of other much-needed religious goods. Besides the Bible, they are authorizing the publication of New Age cult literature, Korans, and Buddhist Sutras.

"But," complained one underground church leader, "the government is so corrupt and greedy now that you can't trust them. They will take your money — and even let you inspect the Bibles — but we Chinese can be very deceptive. You still don't know where the Bibles are going."

However, if the RAB in Beijing began freely licensing Bible publishing as Russia finally did in the last days of the USSR, the Bible shortage could be solved in a few short years.

(4) PRIVATE PUBLICATION — Meanwhile, private publication of Bibles on government and military presses is very risky, but is increasingly attractive to corrupt officials. They see it as another way to make some fast profits to capitalize their factories or modernize the Chinese armed forces.

Underground publishing agents of pornography, pirated computer software, films, music, videos, and other illegal products are sometimes willing to run the risk of printing Bibles as well. This is the fourth method of Bible publishing. It runs hot and cold however — and mostly cold. Brief printing opportunities occur only when press time or paper stocks are available at the same time U.S. dollars are offered. No doubt it would explode into a multi-million dollar publishing business if legal freedom of press becomes a reality in China — or officials choose to look the other way as they do for pornography and computer software copying.

However, private publishing is officially thwarted now by political control of paper supplies and inadequate distribution methods. Transporting and storing truckloads of Bibles is even more impossible than finding press-time. It is very risky and has to be done with meticulous planning — or miraculous intervention by the Lord himself. Transportation bribes and payments also require large amounts of capital in U.S. dollars or other hard currencies.

The most risky and difficult publishing of all is that done on church-owned and operated underground "presses." A handful of antique, hand-operated "proof presses" still exist as do some more modern reproduction methods such as photo-copiers, thermographs, and mimeograph. In addition, scribes still voluntarily hand-copy whole books and pages of the Bible — sometimes from radio broadcasts at dictation speed.

Amateur printing is difficult because even office paper and related printing supplies are licensed and tightly controlled by the government. Yet these heroic underground publishing operations continue and have kept the Word alive in some of the most difficult times of persecution.

Distribution in China Today

The biggest problem in China has never been

printing Bibles, but distribution. All Christian bookstores, retailers, and religious suppliers were closed down at the start of the People's Republic.

Even in pre-Communist China, Christian publishers never had highly developed religious trade associations such as the Christian Booksellers Association or Evangelical Publishers Association in the USA. Bible distribution before the revolution was largely carried on by native missionary "colporteurs" who went from village to village selling scriptures. Denominations, missions, and the Bible Societies supported these itinerant workers.

Today, religious-retailing of any kind remains forbidden in China, and even secular bookstores do not carry religious literature. Nor are there any indigenous direct-marketing catalogs, warehouses, or Christian broadcasters offering literature by mail-order.

The TSPM operates some primitive, institutionally-based distribution centers which offer a very limited amount of Bibles, hymn books, and liturgical aids, or prayer books. These are mostly for clergy and church leadership only. There is little or nothing available for laity — and no one can freely walk in off the street and purchase a Bible or any other Christian publication.

Sadly, no Christian Bibles or books are allowed into the normal retail channels of distribution: bookstalls, bookstores, department stores, newsstands, or variety stores.

China's Multi-Billion Dollar Christian Market

For example nobody even offers Sunday school curriculum, children's books, or youth materials to Christians. Government restrictions still forbid evangelism or Christian education of children. Nor are there men's, women's, or other special program materials for auxiliary groups.

The endless stream of new religious novels, teaching books, and gift items that are a multi-billion dollar annual business in the United States are beyond the imagination of Chinese believers.

Yet the Chinese are zealous in both business and study. Christians are avid readers and hungry for literature. With the second largest evangelical church in the world, it is easy to imagine China becoming the global center of Christian book and Bible publishing. It could happen almost overnight when freedom of the press is restored to China.

I believe it will, too — even if only for short periods of time. That's why Christian leaders and planners should prepare now for the day when freedom of press and broadcasting are restored. Books must be written and translated, graphics made ready, and capital raised now to buy printing plants, distribution channels, and warehousing. House church leaders are praying for the day when the Word of God will again circulate in China as dew falls on the morning grass. We can be confident that God will answer that prayer in the 21st century.

The Dragon Has Not Lost the Battle

While we may think communism is dead, we're kidding ourselves if we think the dragon has already lost the battle against the Bible! The greatest Bible distribution effort in the history of the Church still needs to be organized for China.

It remains for the international Christian business

community to come to the aid of the Chinese with co-venture capital and technical assistance. The profit motive alone should be enough to break down the barriers — but it is not.

There is also a tremendous need for anointed artists, scholars, teachers, translators, and writers who will create a new generation of Christian books, products, and videos for the Pacific Rim. For all this to happen, we need to pray. Spiritual war must be waged against the dragon's control of Chinese broadcasting media, publishing, and retailing. We must bind the strong man of Luke 11:21-22 before the Word of God will go forth in the end-times flood that China needs.

Because of their huge home market, Chinese publishers could build the largest Christian publishing plants in the world. Bible and book import/exports are largely unregulated outside China so this is a natural growth market for the Chinese economy. America's billion-dollar-a-year Christian publishing industry could easily become a five billion dollar industry in China. Furthermore, the new Chinese production facilities could develop into a major source of Bibles and Christian literature for the West as well as the East. But first, Chinese officials must normalize and deregulate the Christian publishing industry in China.

Chancellor Dr. Jerry Falwell (right), of Liberty University in Lynchburgh, Virginia, presents Joseph Lam with an Honorary Doctor of Humanities degree in recognition of Dr. Lam's years of missionary service and for the humanitarian aid given throughout Asia and especially China.

Chapter 9

The Chinese Dragon
and You

*By this all will know that you are My
disciples if you have love for one another
(John 13:35;NKJV).*

Destiny: China's mass of humanity actually faces
two! One is on the bloody battlefields of Armageddon. The second is at the Lamb's banquet-
ing table in heaven. But these eternal destinies depend
on us. What we do right here in the United States will
affect the eternal destiny of over one billion souls.
That's why this final chapter is so critical.

Daily at our international headquarters office in the
USA, my ministry staff and I open letters from very
sincere American Christians. While they may word the
question in many different ways, they are all asking us
basically the same thing, "How can I get more involved

in China?" I would like to suggest seven ways to answer that question.

I believe most of those who write to us this way are actually feeling the Holy Spirit's "end times tug" on their heart-strings for China. They may not understand where this supernatural love is coming from — but it is there — the miraculous seed of divine love for a people who are not their own. How else can one explain America's love of the Chinese people?

If not already "China-lovers" when they write, these American friends soon join the ranks of our "end-times army of love" for China's millions. As the news media fills with stories and pictures of China and her Pacific Rim "tiger-cub" nations, Americans are sensing the excitement of these historic changes. I'm not the only one who senses the urgency of China's 21st century cry for help. God is calling many to join us. They want to help in practical ways — and they're anxious to help right now. Americans are still among the most generous people on earth when you give them a chance.

Are You Becoming One of Us, Too?

Perhaps you sense you are becoming one of the growing numbers of "China friends" in the USA. That's probably why you've read this far. Perhaps you are asking yourself the same question the others are asking me, "Now what? How can I get more involved in China?"

Well, I have an answer for your question — and I hope it doesn't sound like a paradox. The fact is, you don't have to get involved in China! China will get involved in you. If you're an American, you're already more involved than you realize! China is not going away. And the Chinese people are not going away. We're here to stay. We're in your future whether you want us or not."

That has been one of the main messages I've tried to communicate throughout this book. China is no longer waiting for you to come to her — she is coming to you. So the real question is, "Since I am already involved, how should I act toward the Chinese?" Every American, especially every Christian American, needs to answer that question personally. That's why this book could never be complete without a final chapter on "where we go from here."

Dealing with the Dragon

I hope you're in a quiet place as you read these last pages, and that you'll open your heart to God as you read. Let Him speak to you and enlarge your faith. It's time to decide how you're personally going to deal with the dragon.

How are you going to conquer his activity in your own life and environment? How are you going to successfully confront this ancient spiritual force and overcome?

FIRST, SUCCESSFUL INVOLVEMENT IN CHINA BEGINS WITH A HEART-CHECK. It may even involve changing your motivations. For most Americans, it surely means going back to renew the foundations upon which our culture and society was built — reaffirming our own spiritual roots.

To deal with China, America needs a national revival desperately — and I will address that subject again at the close of this chapter. But even before that, it needs Christians who have had a personal revival. I want to emphasize right now that no matter what happens in the USA or in China, something has to be happening in your heart first.

That heart-change will, in turn, translate into specific actions. As business owners, as church members, as family, as citizens and as workers we can adjust to the challenges of New China — but only if we start with the right attitudes. That will renew the "caring ethos" . . . the commitment to humanity that made us great in the first place. The USA didn't become a global power because it had imperial ambitions — but because it loved God's laws, freedom, and justice.

When will we grow up? When will we be mature "parental" Christians again instead of baby-believers? This is a choice that each of us must make in his or her own prayer closet. Revelation talks about it in terms of "overcoming". In the last days, the Bible says there are going to be two classes of Christians: overcomers and casualties. Victors and victims. The choice is in your hands as an individual — and then in ours as a nation.

SECOND, SUCCESSFUL INVOLVEMENT MEANS SHOWING A LOT MORE PRACTICAL CONCERN FOR CHINESE PEOPLE. Harry Wu, the Chinese human rights advocate, was recently interviewed on "All Things Considered," the PBS network news program. It was near Christmas time, and Wu was begging Americans to boycott Chinese-made toys as a protest against slave labor in the torturous "Laogai" prison camps. (These are China's version of the old Soviet gulags. Harry has written about them in his books, *Bitter Winds, Laogai* and *Troublemaker*).

The Public Broadcasting Service interviewer dryly questioned Wu, barely containing his sarcasm. Finally, he turned to Wu with a note of condescension and asked something like this, "Mr. Wu, if we don't buy these cheap prison-made goods, won't the Chinese just sell them elsewhere? Why should Americans care about the condition of laborers in China — what difference will it make anyway?"

Harry came back with devastating sincerity. "Because," he said, pausing between each word, "you are America."

He spoke those four simple words in broken, Chinese-style English. Each word was sounded out separately with the staccato beat of a machine gun. He said it with all the longing of a child looking into a toy store window. It made me proud to be an American. And it underlines an important fact about what's going on today in China. The Chinese pretend they don't care what Americans say, what we think, or what we do about their human rights violations. Yet in reality they are hanging on every word. They are still taking their moral cues from us.

What a powerful reply Wu gave to those who would have us betray the dream of freedom. It was that dream which caused my family to flee China for the USA! America has been and still is "the land of the free." Sure, America has had many problems through the years. We have shameful memories of discrimination, indentured labor, slavery, and segregation. But we repented of these social sins — and came back with reforms, emancipation, and the civil rights movement!

Why We Can't Give Up

These social changes happened, usually rather peacefully, under rule of law in the USA. Why? It's because the American constitution is based on God's commandments for justice, freedom, and righteousness. This country has always sheltered the poor and oppressed because it was founded by Bible-believing men and women. We work to change evils in our personal lives and in society because the Bible tells us so. We can change anything from abortion to slavery because of our faith in God. That is why America is still the world's moral compass. Why China is still looking to us for moral leadership. We must not let them down.

THIRD, SUCCESSFUL INVOLVEMENT IN CHINA REQUIRES PERSISTENCE. Don't give up hope. Americans must not stop fighting for the principles of freedom that made us a great nation. We can't stop preaching the gospel — supporting native preachers. The dragon is a master at protracted warfare. He plans to outlast us, not through his superior strength, but by getting us to quit. That's what his terror strategy is all about . . . wearing down our faith and hope.

So wherever we go to live or do business, we can't give up our Bible-based, faith-based morality. We are involved. When we buy Chinese goods we are partly responsible for slave-labor in China. When we supply the technology and invest our capital, we're helping the system. We have a responsible to resist this evil because we're part of it! No wonder the Red Dragon is on a collision course with American democracy. Satan is just hanging on in hopes that we'll swallow his "big lie" strategy before the crash comes.

"Nothing is going to change in China," he lies with a smile, "and in the end you'll only hurt yourselves and your economy by getting involved. So stop trying to be the world's policeman. Back away and let the Chinese handle their own problems."

Even though he'll lose in the end, he puts up a great front in hopes that he can bluff us into quitting. If we continue to give up our pledge to protect universal human rights. If we keep following the line of least resistance and indifference in China, then we're morally dead as a nation. If we give up now, we'll no longer be the people of our Constitution. We certainly won't be the people of the Book, God's Word. The Lord has blessed this country because its citizens kept a covenant with Him — and the dragon's ultimate plan for the USA is to get us to break that covenant.

Then he can destroy the USA, too. In the end he fully intends to shut down religious freedom here in the States as well as in China! His plan is to destroy the Bill of Rights.

Although Christ came to set the captive free, Antichrist comes to captivate the free. The dragon's line leads back to slavery for both China and the USA. Like the children and grandchildren of the Jewish holocaust, I have to say "never again" to the dragon. We have to resist evil and obey God. We have to resist the dragon and walk in Christ's footsteps.

The Christian Response

Christians cannot follow the dragon's human rights line because it is the way of Cain. When God asked him about his slain brother, Cain replied with a coy question "Am I my brother's keeper?" Implying, of course, that he wasn't responsible for the life and welfare of his brother.

But the Christian answers, "Yes! I am my brother's keeper." Christians are still concerned about our brothers and sisters in China. I know that because every day ordinary Americans tell me so. We are morally troubled about China today — and rightly so — our collective conscience is not clear.

THE FOURTH STEP TO SUCCESSFUL INVOLVEMENT IS LOVE. This is the "agape" love of the Bible, not the emotional love of pop songs and Hollywood. This is charitable love, the kind of love-in-action demanded by the New Testament.

Christ taught us to demonstrate our faith and discipleship through this kind of love. "Inasmuch as you did it to one of the least of these my brethren, you did it unto me." Christ was speaking about the hungry, the naked, the sick, and the imprisoned when He spoke these words in Matthew 25:40-45.

In another place, He said that the people of the world (folks like the Chinese!) will only know that we're His disciples by our love (John 13:35).

When we show this kind of love, God's love, we are using the only force stronger than the dragon's trusty old weapon: fear. The Bible says perfect love casts out fear. It is stronger than his armies. His bombs. His lies. His economic power. The Bible says love is stronger than even death itself.

Love, and only love, melts Chinese hearts of distrust, fear and shame. Friendship is the way to the Chinese heart. This is what has to be the force behind our relationships with China. God is calling America into partnership, not confrontation with China. We resist evil in China, but through friendship. The dragon wants us to resist with hatred and war instead.

The way that American missions in Hong Kong are partnering with indigenous Chinese missions is the model for the future. What's happening to the Church in places like Hong Kong right now is pointing the way to the future. We are finding ways to be accountable to one another without 20th century imperialism — to deliver the Word of God, care for fatherless children, heal the sick, feed the hungry, and proclaim liberty to the captives. This is the ongoing work of Christ's love in the world.

Winning Hearts of Shame

Love is the only way to work successfully within any of the many Chinese cultures. Christian friendship overcomes the barriers of fear and shame between Chinese and Americans. The dragon can't stand against this love from God's people. In the end it is the only hope we have for harmony, justice, peace, and prosperity in the 21st century.

Chinese hearts do respond to loving relationships. In fact, it is the ideal way we Chinese do business — and live our lives. We are a people networked into families and businesses rather than communities. Now we are being networked into churches as well.

SO THE FIFTH WAY TO SUCCESSFULLY INVOLVE YOURSELF IN CHINA IS TO START MAKING CHINESE FRIENDS. Begin as many Chinese friendships as you can. Chinese friendships are involved and accountable. Chinese friends are demanding, and expect you to make demands on them as well. (Remember to introduce your Chinese acquaintances to Christ and the gospel as early as possible in your relationship! Without Christ, there can be little true love or true friendship.)

Where can you go to make these friendships? Here

are four places or "groups" that you can easily visit:

* (1) Chinese students, scholars, and immigrants — Tens of thousands of Chinese have been sent to the United States by the Chinese government to study American culture and science. Few of them have any American friends — and many forces keep them culturally isolated. Even for those who end up defecting and staying here, there are many barriers between them and the dominant culture. Why not reach out to the Chinese and other Asians in your community? There are probably more around you than you think.

All Chinese visitors need and want to learn English. Why not teach English to Chinese newcomers in your community? You can start to make contact through local Chinese pastors, international student ministries at your local university, the Chinese consulate, or the deans of nearby colleges and schools.

Invite Chinese visitors to your holiday meals, special events, and into your home or church groups. Include them in special Christmas, Easter, and Thanksgiving meals and programs. Have Chinese join your next picnic. Eating together is an important way to start and develop friendships in Chinese culture.

* (2) Business, trade, and professional contacts — Work through your own business and professional associations to find Chinese career contacts. Chinese are not "joiners" or club members for the sake of the club, but for the contacts they make. Trade associations may bridge the way to them in your community and overseas. Perhaps civic club memberships will open doors for you in some places. Many service clubs like Rotary and Lions are big on both sides of the Pacific. Include Chinese in your existing business and profes-

sional networks. Make Chinese friends in your field of expertise.

* (3) Exchange visits with China and Pacific Rim countries — Join civic, music, trade, and religious delegations going to Asia, and help host visiting groups from China when they come to your area. I know Americans with cultural interests like art and music who have made lifelong friendships with top Chinese leaders by using hobbies to build bridges in their fields of study.

Cultural exchange visits, "sister city" and "sister church" relationships worked during the cold war to break down many barriers in the old USSR and Eastern European countries. Maybe you can help to renew or start these kinds of bridge-building ministries in your community.

* (4) Working in China — Thousands of Americans are already working in China and in Pacific Rim nations as English teachers, physicians, technicians, nurses, and in businesses of all kinds. Although foreign missionaries are still forbidden, Christian workers who live and work "Chinese-style" are more welcome and needed. Chinese appreciate hardworking, moralistic Americans — although there is still a great deal of discrimination against foreigners and western culture.

American Christians in China face one of the greatest challenges of all, letting the life of Christ shine in the darkness through their actions, lifestyle, and presence. Ask yourself before you go, "Does the light of Christ and His glory shine in my face?" Your body is the only gospel most Chinese will ever read — and it is the first gospel that future Chinese believers will read. Chinese evangelism is lifestyle evangelism.

Other Practical Ways to Show Your Love

While you may have limited personal opportunities to show love directly to Chinese people, there are five other very practical ways that you can still help. These are more indirect ways to show your love for China and Chinese people — but they are ways that everyone can help with immediately.

First, distribute Bibles. There is still an immediate shortage of at least 50 million Bibles among Chinese believers. At least one billion Bibles are needed for the rest of the Chinese nation. Use every opportunity you can to help print Chinese Bibles and personally share them with each of your Chinese friends. I try to carefully offer them to all my Chinese contacts outside official meetings with government or Communist party cadre.

Second, support indigenous Chinese missionaries. Since foreign missionaries are not allowed, sponsor native Gospel workers whenever you can. Chinese missionaries can usually be supported for $30 a month in the countryside — more in the big cities.

Third, adopt and sponsor children, especially orphan girls. The one-child policy has caused the deaths of countless millions of baby girls. Many others are abandoned at birth. Christian orphanages and adoption services are reaching out to save as many of these children as possible. There are also thousands of schools and orphanages in China and the Pacific Rim. They need all kinds of help and sponsors to help raise the next generation of Chinese leadership. There is much to be said for helping save Asian children within their native cultures rather than bringing them to the United States.

Fourth, start sending relief for natural disasters. Many indigenous Chinese Christian relief organizations are now starting up in Hong Kong. They are helping China, Korea and many other Pacific Rim nations with famine, flood, hurricane and refugee relief.

Fifth, support China mission teams. Short-term mission teams and tour groups are sometimes welcome to China. Through goodwill visits to churches and institutions, Bible deliveries, and cultural exchange these delegations are finding new ways to help Chinese church and mission's leaders directly.

If you are interested in supporting any of these kinds of programs, talk with the missions department of your church or write to the mission associations I have listed in the Bibliography of this book. They can supply you with names and addresses of many mission agencies which are involved in those kinds of programs. Finally, you are also welcome to write directly to me at Nora Lam Chinese Ministries International, Box 24466, San Jose, CA 95154. Our mission is involved in all these programs and can channel your support to responsible native leaders.

What to Do When the Dragon Strikes Back

SIXTH, SUCCESSFUL INVOLVEMENT IN CHINA MEANS PRAYER AND SPIRITUAL WARFARE. It wouldn't be fair to paint a picture of an open China that will always reciprocate your love and efforts to reach out in love. The reality is much more chaotic! The doors and windows to China slam open and shut in an almost random manner. You must be diligent, patient, and "ready to go" when the Lord opens a way.

Someday I'll write a book telling how God has given the Nora Lam family victories over the dragon's many attacks — and all the wonderful miracles I have seen. God's grace keeps us going and I am thankful to Him for countless answered prayers.

However, I've learned one thing for sure in all this. Whenever you move out against the dragon — and for Jesus Christ — you will be brutally and unfairly maligned and persecuted. In this world, promised Christ, you will have sufferings along with the victories.

Since the Lord called me into this ministry, I think I have been hit by every kind of attack — but His grace has been sufficient to meet every one. God always has a way out. Before embarking on a China ministry, it is good to memorize the Beatitudes of Christ in Matthew 5. They will comfort you in the tribulations that come with any Chinese outreach.

The dragon is desperately trying to stop the Jesus-advance in China with insidious new strategies. "He is filled with fury because he knows that his time is short" (Rev. 12:12). If he doesn't somehow frustrate our work, he loses his prisoners forever. That means you have a responsibility to be aware "of his schemes . . . in order that Satan might not outwit us" (2 Cor. 2:11).

Watching for the Dragon's Attack

We need to be aware of the dragon's ever-changing anti-Christian strategy of attack. In this book, I have revealed a lot of history about his attacks against Christians, churches, and missions in China. Here's a handy summary of where to expect his counter-attacks when you seek to reach Chinese for Christ:

His first line of defense, stop the warriors. The dragon attacks Christian leaders before anyone else. Whatever it takes, he'll use it against you. He will always hit you personally in your most vulnerable weakness-areas. Beware of any iniquity you have not dealt with as it will open the door for attacks. You can expect demonic oppression, disunity, discouragement, family problems, sin, sickness, and even jealousy and power-struggles from other believers. We've seen it all in our ministry.

His second line of defense, stop the attack. The dragon will frustrate your outreach with closed doors, interference, misunderstanding, persecutions, inadequate help, and poor planning. He'll attack weakness areas of your ministry team, staff, or board of directors. He doesn't fight fair and has no mercy on the foolish or lazy.

His third line of defense, confuse communications. The dragon is a master at false doctrine, half-doctrine, and half-truths. If he can't stop the gospel, he will try to introduce "false gospels" and teachings that get you and your soldiers sidetracked. He will seek to create chaos and disorder through poor communication and even dis-information. Since the Garden of Eden he has specialized in crafty lies (see Genesis 3).

His fourth line of defense, stop our supplies. He counter-attacks where Christ's forces in China and the USA are most vulnerable and sensitive — in their wallets! In fact, I know my very mention of money will turn off some readers or cause them to stop reading this book. But finances in missions are a critical problem today. The cost of raising funds and attracting new supporters for China ministries is enormous. The buying power of the U.S. dollar is shrinking overseas. Americans are giving less to strategic missions and ministries abroad at a time when they should be giving more. Many feel the missions task is done. Many China mission agencies are reconsidering their very existence and future! We have a serious problem.

The China challenge is a wake up call to Americans and American churches. I hope this book will also be that wake-up call in your life — a call to spiritual warfare against the dragon.

This warfare begins with becoming aware and informed. That's why we need to be "pray-reading" every book, broadcast and magazine about China and the Pacific Rim — comparing them with Scripture. God wants us to apply His Word to current events. He wants us to be knowledgeable. He wants us armed and dangerous to Satan. We need to be attacking the dragon rather than be taken by surprise.

For Americans, warfare against the dragon is essentially prayer or prayer-based. It includes other things, but prayer is the foundation. It is something every Christian can do for China everyday. We need to be encouraging intercessory prayer for China as never before. If this book accomplishes nothing else, I hope it gives you a burden to pray for China and America in the times of trial that still lay ahead.

There are prayer maps, prayer diaries, and daily prayer guides available from many ministries to help you pray for China. Please feel free to write my office and we will supply you with a directory of prayer resources to help you pray daily for China including our monthly "Love China Club" newsletter.

Praying five times a day for China is a good rule of life: when rising, at each meal, and finally at bedtime. This will keep you alert to the dragon's counter-attacks.

THE SEVENTH STEP TO SUCCESSFUL INVOLVEMENT IN CHINA IS PROMOTING NATIONAL REVIVAL IN THE USA. As we end the 20th century, there is growing awareness that this is the first century in American history in which we have not witnessed a national revival. I am speaking now, not as a Chinese American — but as an American who loves my adopted country.

I am speaking as a father and head of an American family. As one who loves my children and wants them to inherit the future. I am speaking as one who is just as concerned about the future of my adopted country as I am about my native land.

Past American missions and global outreach has always been provoked by powerful movements of the Holy Spirit in the grassroots of the United States. Past American revivals have always given birth to American missions. We need just such a national revival today if we're going to deal with the dragon as a nation.

We need a collective response. Americans must realize that they're going to have to face the dragon as a nation as well as individuals — and that we're not ready as a nation to take on the 1.2 billion people who are captive slaves to the Red Dragon.

We're overdrawn on our spiritual savings accounts. America is dangerously close to moral and spiritual bankruptcy. Our hospitals and prisons are overflowing as a result. Institutions like marriage and family are disintegrating. Personal moral standards are giving way to a floodtide of avarice, lust, and violence.

So what I'm saying is that it isn't just China or missions that are in turmoil. The "China missions crisis" in the U.S. is only a symptom of the larger moral crisis of a prodigal nation. Time is very short for China and America — but it's not too late. How can I say anything better in closing than to repeat the prophetic promise of 2 Chronicles 7:14? God is still offering America the strength it needs to face the dragon, but we have to accept it of our own free wills:

> If my people, who are called by my name, will humble themselves, and pray and seek my face, and turn from their wicked ways, then I will hear from heaven, and will forgive their sin and heal their land.

Joseph Lam with his mother, Nora Lam,
at Tiananmen Square in Beijing, China.

Bibles for China needed ... NOW!

The U.S. Center for World Missions reports that, "More than 20,000 Chinese people are coming to Christ each day… Revival is sweeping China. The faces of the Christians in this house church meeting have been blacked out to protect their identity.

TOGETHER WE CAN ARM CHRISTIANS IN CHINA WITH THEIR MOST POWERFUL WEAPON… CHINESE LANGUAGE BIBLES.

- - - - - - - - - *CLIP COUPON HERE AND RETURN* - - - - - - - -

BIBLES FOR CHINA

YES, Joseph Lam, I want to help provide Chinese Bibles for the persecuted underground Christians in China. Here is my gift of:

❏ $500　　❏ $250　　❏ $100　　❏ $50　　❏ $25
❏ Other $_____

NAME_____

ADDRESS_____

CITY_____ STATE_____ ZIP_____

Please make checks payable to NORA LAM CHINESE MINISTRIES INTERNATIONAL
and send to: Box 24466, San Jose, CA 95154.   All gifts are tax-deductible.

Bibliography

Any good public library will have a wealth of popular books introducing you to Chinese art, culture, history, and literature such as *The Heart of the Dragon* by Alasdair Clayre (Boston, MA: Houghton Mifflin, 1984). There are also many fine Christian books available, both on the subject of China and end-times prophecy. The following reading list is compiled with the help of China scholar and researcher Tony Lambert of OMF. It is designed to help the reader who is seriously interested in further engaging the Chinese people. However, this bibliography is nowhere near exhaustive. A treasure-trove of old books on China is available in specialized Christian libraries. There are literally thousands of other books and periodicals available. For your convenience, I have divided the reading list into five categories including periodicals. Books marked with an asterisk are especially good for the beginning reader.

I. General Background on China and Asia

Barnett, A. Doak. *Communist China: The Early Years 1949-1955*. Westport, CT: Praeger Publishers, 1968.

Bonavia, David. *The Chinese*. Philadelphia, PA: Lippincott & Crowell, 1980.

*Cheng, Nian. *Life and Death In Shanghai*. London: Grafton Books, 1987.

Clubb, O. Edmund. *Twentieth Century China*. New York, NY: Columbia University Press, 1978.

*Clayre, Alasdair. *The Heart of the Dragon*. Boston, MA: Houghton Mifflin, 1984.

Bond, Michael. *The Psychology of the Chinese People*. Hong Kong: Oxford University Press, 1985.

Fairbank, John K. *The United States and China*. Cambridge, MA: Harvard University Press, 1979. (4th edition)

*Ferroa, Peggy. *Cultures of the World: China*. Marshal Cavendish, 1991. (Sadly, this book seriously underestimates the impact of Christianity on China, but it is very useful as a primary text in most other ways.)

Harrison, J.P. *The Long March to Power: A History of the Chinese Communist Party 1921-1972.* New York, NY: Praeger Publishers, 1972.

Hsu, Immanuel C.Y. *The Rise of Modern China.* New York, NY: Oxford University Press, 1983.

*Jung, Chang. *Wild Swans: Three Daughters of China.* New York, NY: HarperCollins (Flamingo), 1993.

Ladany, Laszlo. *The Communist Party of China and Marxism 1921-1985: A Self-Portrait.* London: C. Hurst, 1988.

Latourette, Kenneth Scott. *The Chinese: Their History and Culture.* New York, NY: Macmillan Company, 1947.

Leys, Simon. *Chinese Shadows.* New York, NY: Viking Press, 1977.

Li Zhisui, Dr. *The Private Life of Chairman Mao.* New York, NY: Random House, 1994.

Liang Heng and Judith Shapiro. *Son of the Revolution.* New York, NY: Alfred A. Knopf, 1983.

Liu, Alan P.L. *How China Is Ruled.* New Jersey; Prentice-Hall, 1986.

*Naisbitt, John. *Megatrends Asia.* New York, NY: Simon & Schuster, 1996.

O'Neill, Hugh B. *Companion to Chinese History.* New York/ Oxford: Facts on File, 1987. A handy alphabetic listing from the Shang dynasty to Deng.

Pan, Lynn. *Sons of the Yellow Emperor: The Story of the Overseas Chinese.* London: Secker & Warburg, 1990.

Salisbury, Harrison E. *The New Emperors Mao and Deng: A Dual Biography.* New York, NY: Harper's Collins, 1992.

Shapiro, Sidney. *Jews in Old China.* New York, NY: Hippocrene Books, 1984.

Spence, Jonathan. *The Search for Modern China.* London: Hutchinson, 1990. Massive but readable account of Chinese history from the late Ming to today.

Terrill, Ross. *China in Our Time: The People of China from the Communist Victory to Tiananmen Square and Beyond.* New York, NY: A Touchstone Book, Simon and Schuster, 1992.

Wu, Ningkun. *A Single Tear: A Family's Persecution, Suffering, Love and Endurance in Communist China*. London: Hodder & Stoughton, 1993.

Post-Mao China

Barme, G. and J. Minford, ed. *Seeds of Fire: Chinese Voices of Conscience*. New York, NY: Noonday Press, 1988.

Butterfield, Fox. *China: Alive in the Bitter Sea*. New York, NY: Time Books; London: Hodder, 1982.

Evans, Richard. *Deng Xiaoping*. London: Hamish Hamilton, 1993.

Frazer, John. *The Chinese: Portrait of a People*. London: Fontana, 1981.

Gardside, Roger. *Coming Alive: China After Mao*. New York, NY: McGraw Hill, 1981.

Hamrin, Carol Lee. *China and the Challenge of the Future: Changing Political Patterns*. Boulder, San Francisco & London: 1990.

Liang Heng and Judith Shapiro. *Return to China: A Survivor of the Cultural Revolution Returns to China Today*. London: Chatto & Windus, 1987.

Liu Zongren. *Two years in the Melting Pot*. China Books and Periodicals Inc., 1984. A fascinating account of a Mainland intellectual's stay in the USA.

Siu, Helen and Zelda Stern, ed. *Mao's Harvest*. New York, NY: Oxford University Press, 1983. A collection of poems, essays etc. by leading Chinese writers.

Mosher, Stephen. *Broken Earth: The Rural Chinese*. New York, NY: Free Press, 1983.

Mosher, Stephen. *China Misperceived: American Illusions and Chinese Reality*. New York, NY: Harper Collins, 1990.

Overholt, William. *The Rise of China: How Economic Reform is Creating a New Superpower*. New York/London: W.W. Norton & Co., 1993.

Zhang Xinxin and Sang Ye. *Chinese Lives: An Oral History of Contemporary China*. New York, NY: Pantheon Books, 1987. Sixty-four interviews with Chinese from all walks of life — fascinating.

National Minorities

Avedon, John. *In Exile from the Land of Snows* [Tibet], London: Michael Joseph, 1984.

Gladney, Dru C. *Muslim Chinese: Ethnic Nationalism in the People's Republic.* Cambridge (USA) & London: Harvard University Press, 1991.

Sinclair, Kevin. *The Forgotten Tribes of China.* London: Merehurst Press, 1987.

Tsering, Marku. *Sharing Christ in the Tibetan Buddhist World.* Upper Darby, PA: Tibet Press, 1988

Religion in China: General

Jiao Guorui. *Qigong: Essentials for Health Promotion.* Beijing: China Reconstructs Press, 1988. Useful book on this cult sweeping China.

Kung, Hans and Julia Ching. *Christianity and Chinese Religions.* New York/London: Doubleday, 1989. Daoism, Confucianism and Buddhism from a Christian perspective.

Taylor, Rodney Y. *The Religious Dimensions of Confucianism.* New York: State University of New York Press, 1990.

Thompson, L.G. *Chinese Religions: An Introduction.* New York, NY: Wadsworth Inc., 1979.

Yang, C.K. *Religion in Chinese Society.* Berkeley, CA: University of California Press, 1961.

II. General Background on Prophecy

*Hagee, John. *Beginning of the End.* Nashville, TN: Thomas Nelson Publishers, 1996.

*Marrs, LaHaye, Breese, Lewis with James. *Storming Toward Armageddon: Essays in Apocalypse I.* Green Forest, AR: New Leaf Press, 1992.

*Arms, Brubaker, Breese, Barela, Carr, Church, Lewis, White and James. *The Triumphant Return of Christ: Essays in Apocalypse II.* Green Forest, AR: New Leaf Press, 1993.

*McAlvany, Breese, Missler, Arms, Sumrall, Church and James. *Earth's Final Days: Essays in Apocalypse III.* Green Forest, AR: New Leaf Press, 1994.

Walvoord, John F. *Major Bible Prophecies: 37 Crucial Prophecies that Affect You Today.* Grand Rapids, MI: Zondervan Publishing House, 1991.

III. Chinese Church and Missions

Current challenges:

Johnstone, Patrick. *The Unreached Peoples*, Seattle, WA: YWAM Publishing. The third book in the "Praying Through the Window" series, it focuses on China and the surrounding areas held hostage by the dragon.

Wong, Ernest, Timothy Lam, Samuel Ling, and Connie Chan. Kingdom Vision and Commission — a reader of the CCCOWE Movement, 1989.

Lawrence, Carl and David Wang. *The Coming Influence of China*, Gresham, OR: Vision House, 1996.

Schneider, Richard. *China Cry: The Nora Lam Story*, Nashville, TN: Thomas Nelson Publishers, 1991.

Christianity in China: Pre-1949

Broomhall. *Hudson Taylor and China's Open Century.* London: Hodder and Stoughton, 1981-85 (seven volumes).

Fairbanks, John K., ed. *The Missionary Enterprise in China and America.* Cambridge (USA)/London: Harvard University Press, 1974.

Covell, Ralph. *Confucius, The Buddha and Christ: A History of the Gospel in Chinese.* New York, NY: Orbis Books, 1986.

Cronin, Vincent. *The Wise Men from the West.* London: Collins, 1984. The life of Matteo Ricci.

Kinnear, Angus. *Against the Tide: The Story of Watchman Nee.* Monterey, CA: Victory Press, 1976.

Latourette, Kenneth Scott. *History of Christian Missions in China.* London: SPCK, 1929. Reprinted, Taipei: Chengwen Publishing Co., 1975.

Lyall, Leslie. *Flame for God: The Story of John Sung* (China's greatest evangelist) Overseas Missionary Fellowship: 1960.

Lyall, Leslie. *Three of China's Mighty Men: David Yang, Watchman Nee and Wang Mingdao.* Overseas Missionary Fellowship, 1974.

Lutz, Jessie G., ed. *Christian Missions in China — Evangelists of What?* Boston, MA: D.C. Heath, 1965. An important compendium of differing views.

Moffett, Samuel Hugh. *The History of Christianity in Asia.* Vol. I. San Francisco, CA: Harper Collins, 1992. Contains over 200 pages on the Nestorian mission to China — the best modern treatment.

Robinson, Lewis Stewart. *Double-Edged Sword: Christianity and 20th Century Chinese Fiction.* Hong Kong: Tao Fong Shan Ecumenical Centre, 1986.

Steer, Roger. *J. Hudson Taylor: A Man in Christ.* OMF, 1990.

Christianity in China: Post-1949

Adebey, David. *China: The Church's Long March.* Ventura, CA: Regal Books, 1985.

Anderson, Ken. *Bold as a Lamb.* Grand Rapids, MI: Zondervan, 1991. Biography of Samuel Lamb, house-church pastor in Guangzhou.

Bush, Richard. *Religion in Communist China.* Nashville, TN: Abingdon Press, 1970. Remains the best documented source for pre-Cultural Revolution Christianity.

Chao, Jonathan. *The China Mission Handbook: A Portrait of China and Its Church.* Hong Kong: Chinese Church Research Center, 1989.

Danyun. *Lilies Among Thorns: Chinese Christians Tell Their Stories Through Blood and Tears.* Tonbridge: Sovereign World, 1991.

Hunter, Alan and Kimkwong Chan. *Protestantism in Contemporary China.* New York, NY: Cambridge University Press, 1993. A balanced overview.

Jones, Francis Price. *Documents of the Three Self Movement: Source Materials for the Study of the Protestant Church in Communist China.* New York, NY: National Council of the Churches of Christ in the USA, 1963.

Ladany, L. *The Catholic Church in China.* New York, NY: Freedom House, 1987.

Lambert, Tony. *The Resurrection of the Chinese Church.* London/Sydney: Hodder & Stoughton, 1991. Completely revised and updated edition: Wheaton, IL: Shaw (with OMF), 1994. Author's M.Phil thesis on the post-Cultural Revolution church. Much documentation.

Lyall, Leslie. *Come Wind, Come Weather.* London: Hodder & Stoughton, 1960; Chicago, IL: Moody Press, 1960.

Lyall, Leslie. *Red Sky at Night.* London: Hodder & Stoughton, 1970.

Lyall, Leslie. *New Spring in China.* London: Hodder & Stoughton, 1979.

Lyall, Leslie. *God Reigns in China.* London: Hodder & Stoughton, 1985.

Although out of print these three books provide invaluable material from an evangelical perspective on the Chinese church in the fifties and sixties.

McInnis, D.E. *Religious Policy and Practice in Communist China.* New York, NY: Macmillan, 1972. Academic source book with many documents (pre-Cultural Revolution).

McInnis, D.E. *Religion in China Today: Policy and Practice.* New York, NY: Orbis, 1989. Many documents. Covers all religions as well as Christianity.

Patterson, George N. *Christianity in Communist China.* Waco, TX & London: Word Books, 1969. Valuable material on the subversion of the church in fifties.

Patterson, Ross. China: *The Hidden Miracle.* Rochester, WA: Sovereign World: 1993.

Rees, D Vaughan. *The Jesus Family in Communist China.* Paternoster Press, 1959. Rare glimpses of an indigenous, communal church.

Whyte, Bob. *Unfinished Encounter: China and Christianity.* London: Collins, 1988.

IV. Human Rights

Moreno, Pedro C., ed. *Handbook on Religious Liberty Around the World.* The Rutherford Institute, 1996.

Wu, Harry and George Vecsey. *Troublemaker: One Man's Crusade Against China's Cruelty.* New York, NY: Times Books, 1996.

Wu, Harry. *Laogai — The Chinese Gulag.*

Wu, Harry and Carolyn Wakeman. *Bitter Winds: A Memoir of My Years in China's Gulag.*

V. Periodical and Prayer Letter Publishers

Amity News Service, (quarterly,) ANS, Kowloon, Hong Kong.

Bridge — Church Life in China Today, (bi-monthly,) Christian Study Centre on Chinese Religion & Culture, Kowloon, Hong Kong. Very useful, covering both "official" and "house" churches.

China Insight, (bi-monthly,) OMF International, Littleton, CO.

China News and Prayer, Far East Broadcasting Company, Kowloon, Hong Kong.

China News and Church Report, (fortnightly,) China Ministries International, N.T. Hong Kong.

China Study Journal, (quarterly,) Council of Churches for Britain & Ireland, London.

China Today, (monthly,) Nora Lam Ministries International, San Jose, CA.

Hong Kong & China Ministry Report, Revival Christian Church, Kowloon Hong Kong (from a charismatic perspective).

OMF *China Prayer,* (monthly,) OMF International, Sevenoaks, England.

Pray for China Fellowship, (monthly,) OMF International, Littleton, CO.

Pray for China, Christian Communications Ltd., Hong Kong.

Tian Feng, (monthly,) Shanghai, PRC In Chinese only; the only officially allowed magazine of the Protestant church in China. Extracts are often translated in *China Study Journal.*

Glossary of Terms

Amity Foundation — A charity controlled by the Three Self Patriotic Movement set up to receive foreign aid. The Foundation owns a press in Nanjing which is used to print Bibles, calendars and other Christian books. It is the only legal Christian publishing house meeting the literature needs of China's churches and believers.

Basic Law — A constitution-style document signed by China the United Kingdom under which Hong Kong will be governed for the first 50 years from 1997 to 2047. It is significant to Christians because it guarantees basic freedoms of religion and press.

China Christian Council (CCC) — An ecumenical organization controlled by the CPC and the TSPM whose stated objective is to unite all Christian believers to cooperate with one mind to further the cause of a self-governing, self-supporting, and self propagating church. The CCC is the only organization allowed to represent the Chinese churches internationally. Traditionally it has been more concerned with pastoral needs of the Churches than the political concerns of the TSPM.

CCP — The Chinese Communist Party, a Marxist political movement which has controlled China since 1949. It follows an atheistic philosophy of secular materialism.

Indigenous — This term is applied to Chinese church and missionary movements that are free from both western and secular political control. It was defined at the Madras Conference of the International Missions Committee in 1938 as follows, "An indigenous church, young or old, is a Church which, rooted in obedience to Christ, spontaneously uses forms of thought or modes of action nurtured and familiar in its own environment."

Laogai — A vast network of more than 1200 prison labor camps used to oppress and re-educate pastors and Christian leaders. The Chinese equivalent of the former Soviet gulag.

Pacific Rim — A popular term used to describe the growing Chinese hegemony in the Pacific basin including all the countries and nation-states whose economies depend heavily on trade with China, including the United States.

Public Security Bureau Police (PSB) — The Chinese equivalent of the former Soviet KGB, an internal secret police force used to oppress Christians. The PSB is frequently the martial force used to enforce edicts from the Religious Affairs Bureau.

Religious Affairs Bureau — A government department in Beijing of the State Council of the CCP Central Committee which also reports to the United Front Work Department. The RAB and its national network of branch offices use the PSB Police to govern the Christian churches. The TSPM, YMCA/YWCA, Amity Foundation and China Christian Council plus all registered churches are supervised by the RAB.

Great Cultural Revolution — A 10-year reign of terror which lasted from around 1966 to 1976 during which all churches were closed and an attempt made to destroy all Bibles.

"Strike Hard" Campaign — A term widely used to describe the current persecution of Chinese churches which began as a result of the follow-up of the Tiananmen Square massacre in 1989.

10/40 Window — A geographical area from 10 to 40 degrees longitude, extending from Japan to West Africa which contains the most unreached peoples of the world. It is the territory controlled by the Dragon. China is the heartland.

Three Self Patriotic Movement (TSPM) — A political "united front" first established by the CPC to organize Christian support for the Korean war. It has since been used to register and organize Buddhist, Catholic and Protestant congregations for the purpose of Communist party control. The "three selfs" are "self-governing", "self-propagating" and "self-supporting".

Where to Go for More Help

If you are interested in supporting Chinese missions, the following associations have updated directories of member organizations who are involved in reaching China and Pacific Rim people groups with the Gospel.

ASSOCIATION OF INTERNATIONAL MISSION SERVICES, Dr. Howard Foltz, P.O. Box 54534, Virginia Beach, VA 23464. Phone (804) 579-5850. (An association of church congregations, independent and denominational mission agencies.)

EVANGELICAL FOREIGN MISSIONS ASSOCIATION (EFMA), Paul McKaughan, 1023 15th Street NW, Suite 500, Washington, DC 20005-1922. Phone (202) 789-1500. (An association of predominantly denominational mission agencies.)

INDEPENDENT FOREIGN MISSIONS ASSOCIATION (IFMA), John Orm, Box 398, Wheaton, IL 60189. (630) 682-9270. (An association of non-denominational mission agencies.)

FELLOWSHIP OF INDIGENOUS MISSION AGENCIES (FIMA), c/o Interim Secretary, P.O. Box 6511, Charlottesville, VA 22906. (This fellowship is the "ad hoc association" of mission agencies that support native missionary movements in China and throughout the Asian Pacific Rim.)

To Contact the Authors

If you wish to contact Joseph Lam or Wm. Thomas Bray, you are welcome to correspond with us c/o Nora Lam Chinese Ministries International, Box 24466, San Jose, CA 95154.